Defining
AMERICA

A Christian Critique
of the American Dream

by ROBERT BENNE
PHILIP HEFNER

FORTRESS PRESS   Philadelphia

Library of Congress Catalog Card Number 73-89062

ISBN 0-8006-1075-X

4063L73   Printed in U.S.A.   1-1075

To those who taught us
To dream the Dream
And to those whose
Questions chastened it

Ultimately a people's religion, no matter how it
has been composed, becomes that people's own
"soul." Whatever inner contradictions it houses,
it serves an essential purpose for those whose
collective consciousness it represented. When
the "soul" departs, as mortals have known since
the beginning of time, the body soon dies too.

Harvey Cox
The Seduction of the Spirit

Table of Contents

Preface

In these pages the reader will come across two American Christians who are in the process of exploring what it might mean to be *both* American *and* Christian one-third of the way through the seventies, the decade in which the United States marks its two hundredth anniversary as a nation and over three hundred years since the Europeans became serious about taking over North America.

The twists and turns of our journey have been perhaps as fascinating and as worthy of reflection as the final goal itself. It has been a journey, thus far, that has moved between two geographical settings—the Midwest guts of the American nation and the German heartland of Europe. Strangely enough, in this most secular of ages, being Christian has often been less problematic than being American. We think of the fellow theologian who somewhat loftily asks, "Why should Christians be interested in making any one a good American?" and the good German friend in Hamburg, a second-generation Marxist, who shouted out in her frustration in the midst of a long political discussion, "Why does it matter to you so much that you are *American*? Isn't it enough simply to be a human being?" This question of *why* we should concern ourselves with our Americanness influences the entire enterprise, but we have not really dealt with it. We couldn't. The brute fact, pressing in our bones, was too real—*How* can we be Americans with integrity? —to allow ourselves the luxury of wondering whether it was proper to have the visceral feelings we did. *How* to be American was the actual question. Whether one *ought* to be American was, for us at least, second-level intellectualizing.

The question that bugged us is the unsophisticated problem, we suspect, that haunts millions of Americans and millions more of our brothers and sisters who are not American. We recognize our kinship with the Philadelphia pastor who asked, when he heard that we were working on this project, "Can you give me some help

in my effort to be *proud* of my country again?" There is the same
bond with the Dresden, Germany, plant manager, who heard us
describe Peter Berger's celebrated theory of the "blueing of America," suggesting that a whole new class of youth with working-
class backgrounds might be in the ascendency in the United States.
A gleam came into the eyes of this low-ranking Communist func-
tionary when he said, "It would be exciting to see America deal
with its capitalistic problems and become a nation that belonged to
the common people."

Our Christianness has been less problematic, even though we
have been barraged constantly by the so-called secularists in community and university. No doubt it is the blend of pluralism and
pragmatism in our society that allowed us to join with persons of
many identities—some familiar, like ours, some truly weird—to
carry on the common tasks of life on the south side of Chicago
where we have both spent the larger part of our mature lives. It
may be a quirk of the graduate school education we received that it
has never seemed anything but obvious that cultural realities and
religious faith would be intertwined, that our Christianness, no
matter how fresh and "revealed" we might consider it in our own
hearts, is in some sense an expression or even flowering of our
Americanness. In the course of the tumultuous decade of the sixties, to which so much of this volume owes its existence, it became
utterly evident to us that our American identity must be seriously
questioned and redirected by our Christian faith. The abstract pronouncements of the neo-orthodox theologians, Karl Barth, Reinhold
Niebuhr, Emil Brunner, who lived through traumatic times that
were only textbook stories to us—these pronouncements of the tension between Christian faith and national identity did not begin to
affect our thinking with the force that the process of simply living
through the decade from 1964 to 1974 in America has.

Our attempt here, however, is not just that of relating Christian
and American identity. Rather, we have tried to accomplish two
things: to say for ourselves that it *is* possible to interpret American
life in the present situation in such a way that one can with integrity participate in America and still be Christian, and secondly, to
spell out the strategy of response which we believe is imperative
for Christians. (We believe that this strategy is imperative for

Jews and secularists, too, but we do not presume to speak for them.) Furthermore, we have sought to make this a genuinely *theological* book, meaning thereby that our reflections are carried out in unabashed belief in God and his presence in our world, and the resolutions we offer here presuppose his active power at work in our history. Since we affirm a classical Christian humanism which, with Saint Augustine and Saint Thomas, believes that Christian faith in God confirms and perfects ordinary human life and thought, it should be quite possible to eliminate our God-talk and find in this book a strategy for being American that any non-Christian might be able to endorse. However, we have no interest whatsoever in hiding the traces of our Christian belief about God and his ways. It is a culturally conditioned and enriched faith that underlies our reflection, but it is a Christian faith through and through.

There is another problem that confronts us. Although we can claim competence in Christian theology, we are less than amateurs in the study of American history and culture. Understanding and interpreting American history and life is *essential* for us, because we are who we are, and the urgency of this task bears no correlation to our competence in American studies. Those who know more about American history than we do will have to check our biased reading of the facts, and they will have to call us to task. We believe they will not find our interpretation hopelessly inadequate. We claim no right to argue its superiority to other interpretations, however, except that it accords with *our* experience as Americans. The point is that we have done for ourselves what every American must do—tried to make sense of what America has been and is now, in the interest of understanding what America might become. We take no little comfort from Sydney Ahlstrom's recent prize-winning book, *A Religious History of the American People.* Concluding 1,095 pages of historical analysis, he writes,

> A history book that comes down to our own time is thus a tantalizing challenge—and an invitation.
> As an active participant in contemporary history, the reader can hardly escape responsibility for seeking to understand his present circumstances. Beyond that, as an observer of continuity and change in the conditions of his own existence, he may exercise the

privilege that Carl Becker underlined when he spoke of "Everyman his own historian." In this exciting role he will soon discover that the American experience does not explain itself. Whether as amateur or as professional, he will be a pioneer on the frontiers of postmodern civilization.[1]

What Ahlstrom says, we have felt to be unavoidably true. At the same time, we know how dangerous the invitation is—"Everyman his own historian"—but it is a danger to which everyone must be open.

This is genuinely a joint work of two authors. We have not agreed in everything. Our disagreements have been sharp enough that we were challenged to work through problems together, to the point where we can live with what the other has written and take full mutual responsibility for the entire book. We cannot help but recall with pleasure how and where the dialogue has taken place for this book. Its roots lie in the farmland of eastern Nebraska, where we went to Midland College and afterward often visited, university studies in Germany during the fifties, at the University of Chicago in the early sixties and the Lutheran School of Theology at Chicago. Talk got serious during the period of detachment we spent together in Germany during 1971 and 1972. The paths of the Alster Park in Hamburg, the university bars of that city, and the coffee houses in the Fruchtallee contributed their beauty and provocation. So did the late evening walks in West Berlin and the hiking paths of the Black Forest. "Middle Europe" and Midwest America, then, have shaped us and this essay. It is sheer coincidence that the sophisticated centers of mind and spirit that lie between have not figured so prominently for us. Whether (to steal a phrase from Sidney Mead) the two parts of our personal world form mountains astride a valley or valleys embracing a mountain in between, we are not quite sure. We do know that they were not bad vantage points for us, and we are grateful that our world has extended at least as far as their dimensions.

R.B. and P.H.

The South Side of Chicago
September, 1973

[1] Sydney Ahlstrom, *A Religious History of the American People* (New Haven: Yale University Press, 1972).

Chapter I

The Foundations of the American Vision

When I first came to this land
I was not a wealthy man
So I got me a shack
And I did what I could
I named the shack "Break My Back"
But the land was sweet and good
And I did what I could.

Traditional Immigrant Ballad

The election of 1976 approaches. Coincident with it is the bicentennial of the United States of America. Within the last four years we have seen the decisive rejection of a candidate interpreted—rightly or wrongly—as embodying a political philosophy alien to the American tradition. As astute an observer as Walter Lippmann saw in George McGovern the recurring Jacobin heresy—that man is naturally good and perfectible; all that needs to be done is the proper manipulation of the environment by the state in order for his perfectibility to be realized. Lippmann thought that the people rightly rebuffed McGovern's quest for the presidency. He voted for Richard Nixon.

After 1972 we saw the victorious candidate—claimant to the true American tradition—embroiled in problems of his own. Allegations of cynical deceptions, dirty play, coverups, and abuse of executive privilege made many Americans wonder which candidate was indeed the best representative of the American heritage. A landslide victory was followed by a landslide of doubts. Skepticism about the candidates of both major parties heightens the drama of 1976.

What will happen in 1976? Will the bicentennial be the occasion for the clarification and purification of the American tradition

1

so that the third hundred years of the nation will be built on a solid foundation? Who will bear the responsibility of setting our politics firmly on that foundation? Or will we shun the tradition and its politics for either a leftist or rightist alternative? Or will we muddle through, relying on Yankee ingenuity and God's grace without any thorough stock-taking of our own?

All of these questions assume that there indeed is an American tradition—a *mythos*, a dream that identifies us as it undergirds our past experience, our present challenges, and our future projects. No doubt there are many American traditions and it is therefore hazardous to point to one, or to a constellation of several that fit together. But there *is* something distinctive about American character and culture. As with all other great civilizations, it too has a mythopoetic motif that runs deeply in its life and is the cultural substratum for its identity and aspirations.

Primal Myth

R. W. B. Lewis, in his classic *The American Adam*, argues cogently that the ongoing dialogue (at times a hot dispute) concerning this American cultural substratum takes place within the context of the primal vision of the American as Adam-before-the-Fall. The American Adam—so the myth goes—is a "figure of heroic innocence and vast potentialities, poised at the start of a new history."[1] Like the biblical Adam before the Fall, his moral position was prior to experience and in his newness he was fundamentally innocent.

This primal myth was what drove the optimistic thought and writing of Whitman, Emerson, Thoreau, Holmes, and Cooper. From the beginning, however, there were undercurrents of a more tragic vision of American life and experience. The elder Henry James, Hawthorne, and Melville explored the darker side of the myth of Adam—his Fall and death. They called into question "the sleek and comely Adamic condition" propounded by the optimists. Lewis argues correctly that the Adamic myth in its unchastened form won the day in the nineteenth century and carried its victory forward into the twentieth.

Lewis's explication of a foundational myth is extremely persuasive and accounts for many of the heights and depths of the American character. He has, however, located only one of the foundations, albeit a very important one. It is the beginning step in a broader myth that includes it. The broader myth is that of the New Israel. The story of Israel includes Adam and his Fall but also encompasses the great stories of Abraham and Moses. Particularly the latter two add further dimensions to the dramatic form that became the American story. In both the Abrahamic and Mosaic stories, the heroes are elected by God, not because of any particular merit of their own but because of God's own goodness. God by his own promises leads them out of the ordered and predictable world of the past, a past that either was or would become oppressive were the hero not to heed the call. Both characters trust in the promise. In trust they move from the past out into the wilderness in which a struggle for new identity takes place. In the midst of harassment, confusion, and difficult conditions, a struggling ascent toward the Promised Land ensues.

Accompanying trust in the promise of God is obedience to the law of the covenant. The promise, and continued trust in it, is contingent upon living up to the demands of God. God's demands rule the internal life of the covenanted people. They prescribe proper worship and just treatment of those included in the covenanted people. As long as the people abide in God's law, they are supported in the present and assured of the future.

Finally, the promised future is fulfilled; the land flowing with milk and honey is reached and land and sons, the contents of the original promise to Abraham, are realized. Through this covenant of trust and obedience, Israel becomes a "light to the Nations." Her destiny is to bring new hope to mankind through her faith in the promise. Thus, there is a movement out of the ordered or mastered world of the past into a wilderness struggle for a fuller identity in the present and finally the reaching of God's promises in the gracious future. In this movement begun by a graceful election and fulfilled in a gracious future, Israel, by her trust and obedience, becomes a paradigm—a beacon—for all peoples and nations.

The image of the New Israel is a recurring one in early American literature and political rhetoric. Perry Miller's work on the Puritans and their "errand in the wilderness" documents the use of the image in that formative strand of American history. The Puritans drove the image so deeply into the American consciousness that more secularized figures like Washington and Jefferson used it in lofty political commentary. For instance, Jefferson's second inaugural speech included this statement: "I shall need, too, the favor of that Being in whose hands we are, who led our forefathers, as Israel of old, from their native land, and planted them in a country flowing with all the necessaries and comforts of life."[2] Here it is clear that Europe is Egypt, America the Promised Land. God has led his people to establish a new sort of social order that shall be a light to all nations.

Robert Bellah recounts the story about the search for a seal for the United States. Benjamin Franklin proposed a seal in which Moses was lifting up his wand and dividing the Red Sea while Pharaoh was overwhelmed by its waters. The motto accompanying the seal was to be: "Rebellion to tyrants is obedience to God." Jefferson proposed a seal with the children of Israel in the wilderness led by a cloud by day and a pillar of fire by night.[3] Both Franklin and Jefferson, heavily influenced as they were by a more rationalistic deism, yet appealed to these biblical images to express their hopes for their new land.

The image appeared consistently in key political moments, even up through the Kennedy and Johnson inaugurals. However, even though the image is a powerful and recurring one, it needed to become more concrete within American history itself. Just as in the history of religions the emergence of close-at-hand earth gods must compensate for the distance of the sky gods, so the Abrahamic and Mosaic myths had to take particular shape on American soil. The story had to be clothed in American garb. And the Abraham of Genesis became the Abraham of Illinois.

Who doesn't know the story? Abe is born in lowly surroundings —a log cabin where he studies by the flickering light of a fireplace. But he is elected to be great and he is obedient to that election. He leaves the past and in a struggling ascent reaches political office where he fails several times. But out of his struggle in the wilderness he achieves the presidency at a significant moment. He guides the destiny of the Union so that it is saved. But he doesn't live to see the Promised Land. He is assassinated and his death becomes the powerful symbol of sacrifice in behalf of the country and others to come.

While there are many other stories that became American versions of the biblical story, that of Lincoln is no doubt the most familiar and evocative. In the process of giving American content to the shape of the biblical story, however, some interesting things were happening. The story became detached from its biblical roots. Although not completely or consistently detached, the story made sense on its own as a powerful myth defining and grounding American experience. The shaking loose from the past, the struggling ascent upward through the wilderness, and the realization of the promise within a gracious, open future—the myth becomes the dramatic shape of the American story. It becomes the American dream. The sky gods Abraham and Moses become the close-at-hand gods Abe Lincoln and Horatio Alger. At times the relation of the sky gods and the close-at-hand is lifted up for purposes of both celebration and criticism. But it is certainly not always necessary. The nation of America can exist independently of the nation of Israel. The people of America can reenact their story without reference to the people of Israel.

The story has its thousands of variations both religious and secular. From the religious side there were ecstatic invitations to the common man weary of the Old World to join the Exodus and move toward the Promised Land. Edward Johnson, in his *Wonder-Working Providence, 1628–1651*, exalts:

> Oh yes! Oh yes! Oh yes! All you people of Christ that are here oppressed, Imprisoned and scurrilously derided, gather yourselves together, your Wives and little ones, and answer to your severall Names as you shall be shipped for his service, in the Westerne World, and more especially for planting the united Collonies of new England. . . . Know this is the place where the Lord will create a new Heaven and a new Earth in new Churches, and a new Common-wealth together.[4]

The secular examples are perhaps even more numerous—the settlers moving across the frontier, the businessmen shaping the first American cities, the inventors and innovators of a later technological age, and finally the heroes in space, the astronauts, prefigured in the lone heroes of the wide open western spaces. Such a wrestler with the American dream as Norman Mailer, grudgingly accepting the fact that it had happened, exclaimed: "The goddam Wasps have put a man on the moon!"

As with any powerful myth, the American myth became, as Lewis puts it, "an enduring model for the actual."[5] As such it functions in the following ways. First it interprets and organizes experience, fitting it into intelligible patterns. The myth first deals with the question: "What is happening to me?" Certainly the American myth has become the story by which millions of emigrants have understood their lives. It has interpreted the pasts and presents of a great majority of American people living now. It deals not only with mobility and success, but it has resources for dealing with suffering and sacrifice, as the story of Lincoln makes so clear. John and Robert Kennedy and Martin Luther King are caught up in the same interpretative framework. When prisoners of war returned from Vietnam, they appealed to the same images to make their sufferings meaningful.

Secondly, the American myth grounds individual or group existence in a reality that transcends their particular experience of existence. It deals with a second question: "In what greater reality am I participating?" For the most part, it answers by affirming: "You are participating in that great experiment in human history, America." And that is no mean answer. As Reinhold Niebuhr has argued, the nation, above all other entities in life, has the most understandable pretensions to ultimacy because of its obvious power, breadth, permanence, and majesty. As a myth grounds experience in a transcending reality, it also tends to unveil levels of reality in the external world and in the human soul that are not accessible except by myth and story. In ritual rehearsals of the American story—such as Lloyd Warner so aptly analyzed in his description of Memorial Day—people are caught up in a history broader and deeper than their ordinary day-to-day existence. Through the ritual, the reality of the common American experience hits them in a way that elicits deep moods and emotions that correspond to the power of that reality. The state funeral of John Kennedy, the pregame and halftime ceremonies of major sports events like the Super Bowl, and the ritualized commentary on significant achievements such as the first human landing on the moon set up in participants and onlookers alike strong resonance with the mythic structures undergirding American life. This deep resonance accounts for the sharp hostility directed at those who seem to disrespect the more obvious symbols of the American myth. The Black Power salutes in the Mexico City Olympics and casual inattention to the national anthem at the Munich games are instances of such disrespectful gestures that elicited strong disapproving responses.

If a myth serves as a model *of* reality by interpreting experience and grounding it in a broader and deeper context, it also serves as a model *for* reality. That is, a convincing myth aggressively makes a claim upon the hearer. It becomes a model for shaping his future life. The American myth operates in many explicit and implicit ways—schools, mass media, literature, music, dress—to lay claim upon the lives of all Americans. It calls people to conform to its shape.

While it may be true that certain segments of American upper-middle-class young people may no longer be interested in the struggling ascent, it would be mistaken to believe that they represent a majority. Indeed, if the upper-middle class doesn't participate in the dream, they will most likely find themselves replaced by more ambitious elements from the lower-middle and middle classes. As Peter Berger has opined, instead of a coming "greening" of America, we may witness an increasing "blueing of America" as the sons and daughters of the working class fill in the vacancies left by noncompetitive WASPS.

The image of success conveyed by the American dream still enters aggressively into the lives of our people. If it is too late to have that success for themselves, many American parents expect it for their children. And they work to make that expectation come true. The children themselves are motivated by a myth that demands that they surpass the level reached by their parents. It may mean simply improving and expanding the family farm. Or it may mean leaving the risky business of father's farm altogether and moving into wage-earning work in town. Or moving from manual work to white collar occupations. Or from an hourly wage to a monthly salary. From the clerk work of the father to a profession for the son. From the housework of the mother to a career for the daughter.

Whether the myth really works out for everyone is of course another question. But it doubtless provides a model for almost everyone. Americans expect mobility and its benefits.

THE SECULAR VERSION OF THE MYTH

The dramatic form of the American myth can be stated succinctly in secular language. It exhorts us to shake free of the limiting past in a struggling ascent toward the realization of promise in a gracious future. This, we believe, is the primal cultural story and is markedly different from myths that operate as "enduring models of the actual" for other cultures.

It is certainly different from those cultures in which there are strong vestiges of what Arend van Leeuwen calls "ontic" myths. The ontic myths have little or no dramatic movement. They are cyclical—new generations simply reduplicate the life of the past generations. Social positions are placed permanently within the cycle. Persons born into them remain in them. The myth sacralizes a permanent and static social structure. There is little expectation for significant change. Tribal societies in Africa exhibit this pattern, as do the older Hindu and Moslem cultures. Although these ontic societies are breaking up rapidly, they nevertheless present real resistance to "modernization."[6]

The American myth's emphasis on individual ascent is also distinctively different from the myths of collective ascent. As a nationalist state, Japan, with its dedication to national glory through economic mastery and expansion, provides a rationale for the energetic Japanese worker, even though he may never rise in his company. The communist states, while providing for individual ascent within a controlled collective order, nevertheless ground the lives of their people in the corporate attempt to "build socialism." Even the nonmobile communist worker participates meaningfully in the socialist myth.

But one would have a hard time convincing the American worker that his dignity is sufficiently enhanced by national well-being. "Building the nation" could not carry him through if he felt he was not bettering himself or his children.

In the following we will sketch the basic moments of the American myth in its secular form. As a formative cultural "story," it enables people to interpret their experience—what is happening to them in their "success" or their "failure." It grounds them in a larger reality, the grand American story, which is the collection of all the individual ascents that it celebrates and encourages. Finally, it provides a secular version of a model for their lives. It calls Americans to conformation with its shape.

When vast numbers of people live their lives out of such a story, we have a secular piety. The myth or story, though secular in form, fosters a life-style patterned after it. The American myth, therefore, leads to a distinct, secular piety.

"To shake free of the limiting past . . ."

Thoreau enjoyed talking of a spiritual molting season. As the snake sheds its old skin and wriggles out with a new one, so the past should be cast off like dead skin.[7] The American experiment in a new land had a chance to attempt just that. So, as Lewis argues, the American saw himself as Adam before the Fall. Free from the baggage, inertias, and corruptions of past civilizations, he could write with a clean mind and heart on a clean slate. Even within the boundaries of the American territory itself, such a stance toward the past was more than a minor note. The most spirited and ambitious cut their ties with the settled, eastern seaboard and plunged westward where a new beginning could be made.

> But the Americans were a new kind of Bedouin. More than anything else, they valued the freedom to move, hoping in their very movement to discover what they were looking for. Americans thus valued opportunity, or the chance to seek it, more than purpose.[8]

As Abraham of old, the American was willing to take the risk in being called out of his "mastered world"—the world of the past —and leave it behind. This acceptance and encouragement of fluidity and mobility are part and parcel of the American character. These qualities enabled people to leave behind the civilization of Europe, the settled society of New England, and later the farming communities of the Midwest. But more important, this stance toward the past allowed people to leave their social-class station in

life. The past of the fathers wasn't binding upon the sons. As Eric
Sevareid, the sage of North Dakota, puts it:

> What was the impulse that pushed and pulled those who came? It
> was simply—change, and it is not given to human creatures in the
> mass to believe that change is going to be for the worse. There has
> been no change in the Old World; no essential, drastic change in
> the relations of man to man for centuries. "America," says Eric
> Hoffer, "is the only new thing in history. . . . What was the
> dream? It was rebirth, the eternal, haunting craving of men to be
> born again, the yearning for the second chance. The New World
> was the second chance. The most illiterate knew it in their bones.[9]

Americans were enabled and expected to leave behind the level of
life that their forebears had achieved or inherited.

This playing fast and loose with the past has entered into American business and industrial life. According to two French commentators, Jean-Jacques Servan-Schreiber (*The American Challenge*) and Jean Revel (*Without Marx or Jesus*), this flexible attitude toward the past is one of the keys to the success of American
business and industry. While large European companies tend to
rely unduly on precedent and traditional methods and practices,
Americans detach quickly from the past and innovate rapidly.

> This *flexibility* of the Americans, even more than their wealth, is
> their major weapon. While Common Market officials are still look-
> ing for a law which will permit the creation of European-wide
> businesses, American firms, with their own headquarters, already
> form the framework of a real 'Europeanization.'[10]

Moreover, this freedom from precedent, this proclivity for innovation shows up powerfully in the cultural sphere. Americans
pioneer in new forms of drama, music, literature, etc. In most
cities in Europe, the kiosks with their notices of cultural events are
peppered with features of American origin.

"In a struggling ascent . . ."

The American, detached from past communities and traditions,
was thrown back on his own inner resources and inventiveness. He

was "an individual standing alone, self-reliant and self-propelling, ready to confront whatever awaited him with the aid of his own unique and inherent resources."[11]

Lewis is describing what Riesman later called the "inner-directed" man. This man keys off his own inner principle, not that of the surrounding society. He has the capacity for self-discipline. He is able to defer present gratification for the sake of the future goal implicit in his own inner principle. His asceticism is not an end-in-itself but rather an instrument toward getting the job done. Thus, the notion of sacrifice is important for the American myth. Struggle implies sacrifice, either for one's own future or for the future of one's children. In certain high moments, sacrifice may entail laying down one's own life for the struggling ascent of the nation. Soldiers who have fought and/or died in wars, the martyred presidents, Lincoln and Kennedy, and social prophets such as Martin Luther King manifest the highest reaches of the sacrifice motif—giving up present happiness for the sake of a hoped-for future.

The inner-directed man, the self-starter, was the only one who could make the struggling ascent. Thus, a strong voluntarist motif inserted itself into the culture and has remained there ever since. Americans are the "can do" people even as Chicago, that most American of cities, is the "I will" city. The strong sense of taking responsibility for one's own destiny with as little dependence on outside help as possible has been and is a valued part of the American character. This strand is not unrelated to the growth and development of innumerable voluntary associations which some political theorists think are the key elements in the American democratic tradition.

President Nixon consciously lifted up the tradition of voluntarism in his second inaugural address, when, in a reformulation of John Kennedy's famous injunction, he said, "In our lives, let each of us ask not just what will government do for me, but what can I do for myself?"

In addition, since specialized learning and traditional crafts were left behind or were not available, a high premium was placed on general intelligence, or practical versatility. Boorstin, for instance, indicates how the early business and industrial innovators were geniuses, not in skill and technical knowledge, but in know-how, in general organizing competence to make anything.[12]

Servan-Schreiber argues that this quality has not left the American character—either in its individuals or its businesses. He locates the gap between American and European businesses in a European lack in the art of organization—in the mobilization of practical intelligence to release individual initiative, to promote teamwork, to streamline and decentralize decision-making processes.[13]

In the American myth the ascent will not be easy. Tough competition is the American way. Under competitive circumstance not only will the best win out but the best will be brought out of each competitor.

The race is an evocative metaphor for many Americans. Again, Mr. Nixon illustrates his adherence to the myth when he asserted in a campaign film some years back that every person has a right to get to the starting line in the great American race, but each must run the race for himself. Society owes every person a place at the starting line, he said, but no one should get special help in the competition nor should anyone have special hindrance. Black spokesmen have responded positively to this imagery, generally opposing the welfare state, but insisting that blacks begin the race way behind the starting line and thus need special effort if they are to compete on equal footing with whites.

So, the tasks before the ascending individual and group are great. But the important point is that there is a strong expectation that one can and will ascend with the proper initiative, discipline, and know-how. To be an American means that struggling ascent. When it happens it reconfirms the myth.

"Toward the realization of promise in an open, gracious future . . ."

If there is any sure thing in the American myth it is that the struggling ascent will be enveloped by a gracious future. It will open its doors to those who are struggling upward. As Boorstin says it: "America lived with the constant belief that something better might turn up. Americans were glad enough to keep things growing and moving. When before had men put so much faith in the unexpected?"[14] The doors would open to him who knocked.

The future was not only gracious; it was also open. It was open in two ways. First, there was apparently limitless geographical space. If the present settlement did not please a man, he could always move on to the next horizon and try again. There was elbow room for every free spirit.

But because there were so few people in such a great land, and because it was basically undeveloped, there was also seemingly limitless social space. There was room at the top of the social ladder; there was plenty of room in the middle. And, indeed, there was ample room at the bottom too. The American found his level according to his ability and desire. Classes were fluid and one didn't bump into others either on the way up or on the way down. The channels of mobility were open.

The geographical and social horizons were open. There was room for every dream that was projected onto that open future. In short, there was opportunity. As Boorstin shows, this openness provided the context for the realization of the grandest dreams—some of the early builders of midwestern cities were not content to build just one city. They moved on and developed several. Indeed, the land was not only sweet and good; it was breathtakingly open.

What was and is the promise to be realized in the open, gracious future? Eric Sevareid remarks:

> There were a thousand varieties of finite dreams within the one encompassing dream. Many of the poor came dreaming to be rich; many of the rich, dreaming to be richer. The energetic came, eager to put their hands to work; the lazy hoping to live with no work at all. The God-conscious came, expecting to find Him speaking to them directly, the message ungarbled by official interference. The weak were sure they would become strong, the fearful were certain of confidence. Thieves dreamt of easier thieving; roughnecks wanted more room to swagger; the sick sought health, and from the new air and light and waters and herbs and drugs, the ugly would surely be transformed with beauty. And the apostles of brotherhood came, ignoring the teachings of the sages about the dual, good and evil, nature of man, seized with the lofty and ludicrous notion of Jean Jacques Rousseau that civilization had corrupted man, instead of the other way around. And that, restored to a "state of nature," man would be automatically tolerant, loving and peaceable.[15]

No one can be too certain about American goals. As a nation its goals have never been spelled out. The tradition of the country dictates that no one can or should lay out the goals for anyone else. So, a plurality has ever been the case. Many immigrants came in accordance with the Old Testament promise, land and sons. Others came after the horn of plenty. As Hannah Arendt observes, the dream of the poor masses of Europe who came to these shores was the poor man's dream, a dream of material paradise. Some of more aristocratic bent came to establish free public space in which they could shape their own political destiny. They were interested in "public happiness." Others came for private liberties, freedom *from* coercion in the realms of religion, speech, and association. Perhaps many came for the sheer adventure of it all. And certainly, as Sevareid indicates, many came for the opportunity to achieve success, to win in whatever endeavor they chose. These options, with many more variations, remain as the ends of the struggling ascent. It is extremely dangerous to generalize about the goals of Americans. Even those twin devils, production and consumption, don't account for the deeper aspirations of most of the middle classes whom we think are mad consumers. They have more sophisticated and complex—and for that matter, more profound—notions of the "good life" than radical critics attribute to them. They increasingly pursue fuller interpersonal relations, more significant work, and a freer expressive life.

Shooting through the whole panoply of ends is the implicit belief that there is adequate opportunity for their realization. The doors open and will continue to open for those who shake the limitations of the past and who through self-initiative make the struggling ascent. In summary, then, the social model which follows from the American myth lifts up the values of freedom, initiative, and opportunity. Freedom means freedom from the constraints of others or the past.

> The American social revolution's coat of arms bore and bears one word—Freedom. Not the freedom of a region or sect or point of view. Just freedom, the condition in which a man feels like a human being, like himself. It is the purpose, the definition, and consequence of rebirth. It is The Dream.[16]

Initiative points to the inner-directed effort at ascent, and opportunity refers to an open and basically gracious future.

The myth leads to libertarian democracy over against equalitarian. Not that equalitarian strains are not present in the American tradition. But the dream has assumed that, due to the open geographical and social space, equal opportunity is in fact a reality for those who want to advance. Equality and opportunity, though highly valued and explicitly promised, have generally been unplanned and unintentional. They reside in the openness and graciousness of the country.

The values of freedom, initiative, and opportuntiy not only apply to individuals. They also relate to private groups, corporations, and even the nation itself. Ethnic groups, voluntary associations, business companies, and the national interest are all assumed to have the freedom, initiative, and opportunity to realize their projects in a basically gracious future. They are all involved in the dream. And because America has been true to the promise in the dream, its destiny is to shine forth as a light to all nations. All nations and groups of men can emulate the shaking free of the limits of the past, the struggling ascent, and the movement into a gracious future.

First and foremost, America is the land of liberty. That is what the statue in New York harbor has symbolized to the American people and to the world. It has meant the unfettered exercise of the human spirit within the context of freedom and opportunity. Philosophically speaking, America has lifted up the dynamic potentialities of human life rather than the forms and traditions around which humans have arranged their lives from time immemorial. The myth has moved toward dynamic freedom rather than traditional form; innovation over precedent; aggressive thrust over respectful receptivity; energetic seeking over grateful bestowal; and a celebration of independence over the awareness of dependence or interdependence.

If indeterminate spirit is one of the qualities that make humans truly human, then that spirit has found its energizing myth and gracious environment most fully in America. Perhaps that is the transcendent meaning of the American experiment. Where else have so many been able to exercise their finite freedom without damaging restraint from class and status restrictions, religious intolerance, governmental dictums, or ethnic prejudice? America has taken the risk of human liberty. It has been a sacrament to human longings in the sense that it has allowed a dimension of the truly human—finite freedom—to shine forth *through* a particular human vessel. As such a vessel, America does have transcendent religious meaning.

LIMITING AND SUSTAINING CONTEXTS

From the beginning of our history, the thrusting, ascending spirit into open social and geographical spaces has been embraced by what we shall call limiting and sustaining contexts. If the American myth provides the dynamic upward thrust, these limiting and sustaining contexts provide a surrounding environment of inclusion, accountability, and substance. Though doubtless, as we have argued earlier, the dynamic qualities predominate over this surrounding environment, it has been utterly necessary as a nurturer and conditioner of the ascending centrifugal impulses of our society.

Gibson Winter, in a paper on "The Question of Liberty in a Technologized World," points to this same reality when he lifts up *belonging* as an indispensable counterpart of *liberty*. His elaboration of *choosing* roughly parallels what we have delineated as the meaning of the American myth. But without the other side of the polarity—belonging—choosing becomes empty and finally nihilistic.

> However, it is becoming clear in probing further into the possibilities of a human future, that belonging reaches into the center of the question of liberty. Individual and social initiatives, in fact the whole realm of the voluntary seems inextricably bound up with interdependence and belonging. . . . I am proposing that belonging and choosing comprise together and inseparably the central meaning of liberty.[17]

The notion of "belonging" can be broken, at least in our view, into the two functions we have proposed—limiting and sustaining. By limiting contexts, we mean rules, laws, promises, tacit agreements, countervailing forces, organizational actions, and interventions that hold self-initiating individuals and groups accountable to realities outside themselves, i.e., to God, to the nation, the public good, other competing interests. They serve to mitigate the claims of the strong against the weak and to include the weak in the interaction of the society.

H. Richard Niebuhr, in his *Radical Monotheism and Western Culture*, asserts that a paradox of human life is that those realities that limit us are the same realities that sustain us. He goes on to argue that it is through limiting and sustaining action that God orders and governs his world. But that is getting ahead of ourselves. It is enough to say at this moment that contexts which limit us are also contexts that sustain us. Our spouses and our children or parents limit us, but they are some of the richest sustaining realities in our lives. Nature limits us but also sustains us like a mother.

Every initiative, be it individual or corporate, must come from somewhere and some time. That is, its roots in time and space make it particular. The particular social contexts from which initiative arises give the initiator identity. They bestow *being* upon the actor. No one, even though he may shake off the limits of the past, can shake off his rootage in the past. Of course, we are not arguing that these roots are not being threatened by our emerging mobile, mass society. While threatened and becoming weaker, they are still there to a greater or lesser degree. Without them there would be no identity at all, no being at all. One cannot have, at least in the human world, sheer dynamic without form and substance rooted in the structures of being. Without belonging, no being.

Some of the contexts that sustain us are the "givens" of our lives. We did not choose them. But nevertheless they sustain us and give us identity. We "belong" because of them. Certainly we did not choose the land and culture of our birth. Nor did we choose the family to which we were born. Likewise, we did not choose the religion—or lack of it—that we received as infants. We as finite human beings are "thrown" into many of these contexts of belonging, for better or for worse. Regardless of how much we strive to transcend them, it is constantly surprising, upon reflection, to realize how much of the conditioning of the past we bear forward into our own lives and into the lives of our children. This is true about the conditioning characteristics of our nation, our culture, our church, and our region. Moreover, we are becoming increasingly aware that one of the givens of life that limit and sustain us is the fact of our existence on this "spaceship" earth. Our consciousness of finite amounts of water, air and land—and our dependence on them—grows as we move through time. The human natural condition itself is something we bear with us and for which we must care.

There are also sustaining contexts—to which we belong—that are more involved with our own volition. We choose to belong to them. Even when we submit to the influences of others, we exercise our will by default. We decide whom we will marry, how many children we will have, and how we will raise them. We choose where we will live as we enter adulthood. We join the voluntary organizations of our choice. We decide upon our life's work. Indeed, we may even choose the country where we wish to live. Thus far, however, we have not been able to choose our planet. Most of these contexts of belonging are in conscious or unconscious continuity—sometimes via the route of rebellion—with the givens of our early lives.

Together, our sustaining contexts—whether we choose them or not—make up our identity. Without the particularity of their substance we would not belong. We are never human-beings-in-general, but rather particular humans with concrete identities. When we are divested of our concrete "thatness" we experience rootlessness and, finally, despair. What's more, we become likely targets for manipulation by others.

In the following we will examine our limiting and sustaining contexts under three rubrics: political, social, and cultural. On all three levels there are conditioning environments that hold individuals and groups accountable and that bestow identity on those individuals and groups.

The Political

Perhaps the most important limiting context established in the American political realm was grounded in the natural rights philosophy. The God of the Enlightenment revealed his will in laws and rights that were ascertainable by the exercise of reason. These natural rights and laws were considered to be expressions of the objective order of things and America was to be built in the image of such an order. The great locus of such a belief is of course in the Declaration of Independence:

> We hold these truths to be self-evident, that all men are created equal, that they are endowed by their Creator with certain unalienable Rights, that among these are Life, Liberty, and the pursuit of Happiness—That to secure these rights Governments are instituted among Men, deriving their just Powers from the consent of the governed. . . .

On the one hand, this political philosophy emphasized and reinforces the voluntarist tendencies of the American myth. As Carl Becker has written:

> And so we arrive at the central idea of the natural rights philosophy in respect to the function of the government and the freedom and responsibility of the individual; the happy idea that the best way to secure the inalienable rights of man is just to leave the individual as free as possible to do what he likes, and that accordingly no form of government can secure them so well as the one that governs least.[18]

But there are also powerful affirmations of belonging and limitation inherent in such an approach. First, any person who is an American *belongs*—at least in theory—in the sense that his rights of life, liberty, and the pursuit of happiness ought to be protected and insured. The revolutionary potential of such a declaration is still somewhat breathtaking. It presses for the inclusion of all human beings in the American dream. (Of course the inconsistencies of application in regard to Indians, women, blacks, and Chicanos are from our vantage point notoriously evident.) Also, public and private powers are *limited* in their relation to individuals and groups. There is a limitation on arbitrary power by the separation of powers in government itself and by constitutional guarantees of freedom of speech, association, religion, etc. Thus, tyrannical concentrations of power—public and private—are limited. (In the Watergate and Ellsberg episodes we saw the limitation belatedly taking effect; also in the congressional limitation of bombing in Cambodia.)

A more concrete—in contrast to the natural rights philosophy—approach to the notion of limitation is found in Number 51 of *The Federalist*.

> This policy of supplying, by opposite and rival interests, the defect of better motives, might be traced through the whole system of human affairs, private as well as public. We see it particularly displayed in all the subordinate distributions of power, where the constant aim is to divide and arrange the several offices in such a manner, as that each may be a check on the other—that the private interest of every individual may be a sentinel over the public rights.[19]

And for the relations among different systems:

> It is of great importance in a republic not only to guard the society against the oppression of its ruler, but to guard one part of the society against the injustice of the other part. Different interests necessarily exist in different classes of citizens. If a majority be united by a common interest, the rights of the minority will be insecure. There are but two methods of providing against this evil: the one by creating a will in the community independent of the majority—that is, of the society itself; the other, by comprehending in the society so many separate descriptions of citizens as will render an unjust combination of a majority of the whole very improbable, if not impracticable. ... The second method will be exemplified in the federal republic of the United States.[20]

These principles that prescribe intentional balancing—and therefore mutual limitation—of power centers are built on more pessimistic notions of human nature than the rights of man philosophy. The authors no doubt had some inklings of the darker side of the human spirit than that encompassed in the American myth.

The rights of man philosophy and Federalist prescriptions both have set up the "rules of the game" which order the interplay of self-initiating individuals and groups. As a set of limitations—to which all officeholders and citizens pledge themselves—they are indispensable to both order and justice in our tradition. Even as salty a voluntarist as Saul Alinsky, who never was known to extol ethical and legal rules, admitted on occasion that community organization could survive only if the rules of the game were observed by the broader American society. Without the freedom to associate and organize, the community organization movement could go nowhere. Even with them it is no easy task.

Besides the formal and written rules there are tacit understandings that govern the delicate political balances. Walter Lippmann has reflected on this issue:

> While there obviously has to be some kind of executive privilege, it must be used with the utmost discretion and restraint. Our system of government will simply not work if any principle is pushed to an extreme. There must be respect for the rules on the part of everybody—the President, the Congress, the courts. The men who wrote the Constitution were rational gentlemen. They knew the system they were devising could not work unless the rules were respected. Their primary assumption was that the kind of people who were running the government would play by the rules. If the President refuses to do this, nothing works, and you don't have our constitutional system. The President is actually a king with all the powers and all the limitations inherent in a king. What is important is that there be respect for the unwritten law, which is an important part of the American constitutional system.[21]

Another motif of belonging that limits the anarchy of free ascent and sustains the structure of human communities came to us from the Puritan tradition. The Puritans of course contributed mightily to the forging of the primal American myth that we described earlier. Their errand into the wilderness was indeed a shaking free of the limits of the past and a struggling ascent into an open, gracious future. The stories of Abraham and Moses provided key images to interpret their own experience in this New England.

Upon closer inspection, the three movements of the American myth not only correspond to the movement of Abraham and Moses to the Promised Land; they also correspond to key aspects of the Protestant Ethic, as it was delineated by Max Weber in his *The Protestant Ethic and the Spirit of Capitalism*. Weber argued that the Protestant was sprung free of the traditional conduits of grace —the church, the priesthood—by the doctrine of predestination. A

man's election was something between God and him; the intervention of human institutions made no real difference. So, he was cata-
pulted out of dependence on traditional institutions and communities. He was set free from these limiting and sustaining contexts.

As a free individual, Weber's Protestant was a disciplined, anti-
sensual striver. Because of the Calvinist—and later, Puritan—emphasis on the prohibition of idolatry, the sensuous, sacramental,
and colorful dimensions of the traditional Catholic faith were
rejected. Protestantism took on an iconoclastic, ascetic character.
But this asceticism wasn't relegated to the monastery as in prior
ages. Rather it was wedded to hard work in the secular world, for
it was in one's worldly calling that one glorified God. So, according to Weber, "inner-worldly asceticism" was born. From our
point of view, this provided the religious underpinnings for the
struggling ascent.

Finally, the movement to an open, gracious future in the American myth assured that each struggling ascent would be received
kindly by the future. As the Protestant Ethic had it, disciplined
and ascetic work would be rewarded by worldly prosperity as a
sign of election. Thus, in the New World the Protestant Ethic
came to fruition. The gracious, open, social, and geographical environment beneficently enveloped the struggling ascent. Prosperity
was the reward of virtue.

So, we can see how powerfully the Puritan tradition contributed
to the formation of the primal myth. The cultural characteristics
forged by this potent tradition lived on with great momentum even
after the religious roots were cut off from them.

However, it would be folly not to point out the contributions of
this tradition to what we have called the limiting and sustaining
contexts that surround the myth of ascent. The Puritans were certainly not simple apostles of freedom. They had deep resources in
their faith for limiting that freedom and for constructing communities that provided meaningful contexts for freedom.

H. Richard Niebuhr, in his *The Kingdom of God in America*,
has admirably described these two aspects of the Puritan heritage.
The belief in the absolute sovereignty of God contributed greatly
to the notion of limitation—the limitation of individual freedom,
and of political and religious authority. Radical monotheism meant

the relativization of all human values, institutions, and claims. Nothing was absolute, save God's will. "The converse of dependence on God is independence of everything less than God."[22] Governments and their policies are subordinated to God's will. The authority of churches is limited by a transcendent criteria.

Combined with this insistence that only God is sovereign was the awareness of man's tendency to make something less than God absolute. Man has a sinful propensity toward what Niebuhr called "henotheism"—the elevation of one god among the many—or "polytheism"—the elevation of many gods who constantly war with one another. Thus, in the Puritan tradition there was a sharpened consciousness that the struggling ascent of the individual, corporation, or state was always infected with a self-centered will-to-power. They all had tendencies to claim more than they ought. Therefore, they had to be limited, not only because of their sin but also because of the final sovereignty of God alone.

> The Puritan sought limitation by means of constitutionalism, the Scriptures and "political covenants" and by the dispersion of power; the separatist and Quaker sought it by learning the humility of Christ. Though both ways led to a kind of democracy it was democracy of a sort different from that which marched under the banner of the sovereignty of man. It was democracy subjected to the kingdom of God.[23]

While this tradition of limitation lives on in the various inheritors of Puritanism, and in other Protestant, Catholic, and Jewish communions, it also exists in secular form in the libertarian and anti-authoritarian character of the American people. Outside authorities as such have no overwhelming weight for Americans unless they voluntarily have given their respect to them. The German respect for *Obrigkeit*—authority—is not a predominant trait among Americans. Americans adopt the "show me" stance, which is a relativizing force before all claimants to authority. This "individualism," of course, can lead to a dangerous erosion of any authority whatever, a pitfall that certainly wasn't a fault of our Puritan fathers.

The Puritan tradition had resources for limiting the free ascent of individual and corporate entities. People could belong to the commonwealth without fear of arbitrary intervention of private and public powers. Because of these contexts of limitation, the Puritans could dwell together in concord.

But limitation was not the only means by which the Puritan tradition achieved a measure of belonging. The notion of a "covenanted" people provided a sustaining context that went beyond limitation. It provided the structure for a common life, for a life together under the rule of God. Through the covenant a life-style was shaped that included a harmonious way of relating to man and nature.

As for Abraham of old, the promise of a gracious future for the Puritan was dependent upon obedience to the law of God. Men covenanted themselves to this law which gave order and substance to their lives. It provided for moral ways of relating to each other, to just ways of dealing with both insiders and outsiders, and a respectful mode of relating to nature. The assent to covenant together was a promise to live according to the Kingdom of God already in their midst.

Again, H. Richard Niebuhr says it well:

> This kingdom of God was not something to be built or to be established nor something that came into the world from without; it was rather the rule which, having been established from eternity, needed to be obeyed despite the rebellion against it which flourished in the world. . . . The Puritans, Pilgrims, with their associates, were first of all loyalists. They were loyal, in Chesterton's phrase, to the "flag of the world." They were convinced that this flag represented power and law as well as benevolence in which men could trust when they lost confidence in their own good will and in that of their ecclesiastical and political overlords. To think of them as primarily protestors and rebels is to regard them from a point of view foreign to their own. They were nonconformists, dissenters, protesters, independents, only because they desired to be loyal to the government of God, and in that positive allegiance they were united, however much their unity was obscured for later times by their party quarrels.[24]

The tradition of covenanting ourselves to the objective laws of justice and morality has persisted, sometimes in outright religious form, at other times in secular clothing. There has been an ongoing belief that if a gracious future is to be ours, we must order our lives morally and justly. To belong to America has implied this covenant for one's own life. It has also provided the basis upon which we make sure others belong. Obedience to this covenant has been behind the movements toward "social redemption." It has emerged in the abolitionist movement, the social gospel, and in public figures that have been influenced by it—both Roosevelts, Wilson, Johnson, King, McGovern, to name a few.

The hope of the American future is dependent, in this continuing Puritan tradition, upon the promise we as Americans make to the principles of a just and orderly internal life. Only by our promise-keeping in relation to such an internal life can we maintain the sense of belonging for ourselves and others.

These three strands—the natural rights philosophy, the Federalist prescriptions, and the Puritan heritage—have provided a measure of belonging for Americans. They have provided ongoing contexts of limitation that have tempered the more unruly and centrifugal impulses of the American myth. In so doing they have been instruments of inclusion for those who were on the outside of the society looking in. They have also bestowed a sustaining context in the sense that they have shaped and ordered our common life. They have given substance to our identity as Americans. Even those who are pessimistic about American possibilities make their judgments about our performance primarily in the light of these three strands. To be an American means to subscribe to these political contexts of limitation and sustenance. They are the fertile ground of belonging from which the free ascent takes place.

Although it applies to the social and cultural levels of American life as well as to the political, the concept of the civil religion is most appropriately discussed under the political rubric. In his classic essay entitled "Civil Religion in America," Robert Bellah reclaimed the notion of a national religion that serves as a point of guidance and criticism for American life.[25] It has been the general custom among Jewish and Christian religious thinkers to castigate as vigorously and thoroughly as possible any notion of a national religion. They have tended to see national religion as innocuous, religion-in-general, or as a secularized and bastardized heathenism, or as a downright evil instrument of American interest that is used to legitimate whatever America wants. In any case, the evaluation of civil religion has been consistently low. (Perhaps Sidney Mead's defense of the "religion of democracy" is one of the few exceptions.)

The import of Bellah's influential article is that it has been a powerful witness to a culturally borne religion that has genuine transcendent qualities in it. Our most significant political leaders have drawn upon this religion, an amalgam of biblical and Enlightenment notions, as a point of transcendent critique by which they have summoned the people to a greater realization of their own aspirations. Of course—and Bellah admits this—there are perverted versions of the civil religion that are used to legitimate venal, bizarre, and even evil causes. It can, like all religions, degenerate into a handmaiden of narrow interest.

The civil religion, however, may be a misnomer in the sense that when Bellah uses the term he refers primarily to the *articulated* notions inherent in the practice of civil religion. As such, it is more like a civil *theology* that is the point of critique for the civil *religion*. As in other faiths, religion refers to the full practice of a faith—its rituals, its moods, its perceptions, its ethos—while theology refers to the articulated concepts that both flow from and guide religious practice itself.

But, for the sake of clarity, let us continue to use the civil religion to refer to the articulated constellation of American religious symbols and concepts that derive from the biblical and deistic traditions and serve to gather together the strands of American identity. As such the civil religion carries sacral legitimation for both the American myth and the limiting and sustaining contexts we have just discussed. It grounds both the choosing and belonging poles of American life.

As we argued earlier, the American myth, even in its secular version, promotes and confirms some of the deepest aspirations of the human spirit. The exercise of the free, indeterminate spirit is one. The longing for opportunity for all is another. The posture of optimism about a gracious future is yet another. All of these promptings of human hope and aspiration find their grounding and fulfillment in transcendent reality. At crucial moments the civil religion grounds the aspirations of the human spirit that are inherent in the American myth. At other crucial moments it also holds the American reality—the faulty piety itself—up to the ideals of the American myth and points out the incongruity between real and ideal. In these ways it serves as both transcendent ground and judgment.

The civil religion operates in the same manner in regard to the limiting and sustaining contexts. It provides the legitimation for what Walter Lippmann has called the "public philosophy"—the shared belief that the rules that order our life together are grounded in a moral order that transcends mere national life. It gives authority to the covenant implicit in American life.

Thus, the civil religion spreads its sacred canopy over the American dream of ascent as well as the rules of the game that govern the ascent. It broadens the context of both the dream and the rules. It claims that they have a transcendent referent that is true not only for Americans but for all. The canopy not only bestows sacral legitimation but provides a transcendent point of judgment of our performance. It judges and criticizes our life as well as affirms it.

The civil religion, though, needs constant renewal from sources outside itself or it becomes a mere reflection of American life. For its own health it needs the continued input of concrete Christian and Jewish communities that are anchored firmly in their own authentic traditions. They must provide the ground and judgment of the civil religion itself, lest it fall into a blind idolatry of its own. One of the tragedies of the present situation is that the civil religion has no real spokesman in power or close to power. Billy Graham seems only able to affirm the lesser virtues of the American myth; he seems utterly punchless when the prophetic judgment inherent in the civil religion is called for.

The Social

The American reality can never be exhausted by dissecting the political level. Below the high-level and distant centers of power are the intermediate social units that play so important a role in providing the belonging dimension of human existence. These social units both limit the more distant powers, i.e., hold them accountable, even as they bestow identity upon the people who participate. As such they must be included in our discussion of limiting and sustaining contexts. They provide and preserve the structural and substantive environment from which the American dream thrusts istelf upward.

Perhaps the most important of these are the organic social realities that play more a sustaining than an accountability role. Ethnic groups, neighborhoods, small towns, regions, and extended families all give substance and identity to the lives of people. No doubt mobility and mass society are threatening these sustaining contexts. But perhaps many more people live amid these structures even now than is surmised. Indeed, many studies have indicated that various strands of ethnicity, localism, and regionalism have not melted as quickly or as much as theorists of mass society have argued. (Michael Novak and Andrew Greeley seemingly never tire in pointing to and celebrating the persistence of ethnic identities.)

In addition to the organic social units that enable us to belong, there are the more intentional social institutions that provide a significant share of American identity. Schools, colleges, and universities are but a few examples of the structures that not only launch us on our ascent but also give us lifelong identities that root us somewhere and in some time. The fact that both authors of this present book have sprung from the same small church college where they were influenced by the same teachers and traditions gives them much in common that not only stabilizes their identity but also shapes a certain vision of the world.

We certainly cannot neglect those most intentional of social associations, the voluntary organizations that dot the American social and geographical landscape. Besides giving substance to a person's identity—a Presbyterian layman, a Lion, a member of the ACLU or the NAACP—they provide the society with foci of responsibility and accountability. They are important centers on the intermediate level that limit the intervention of large centers of power into the affairs of the people. Their functions are significant and numerous, and have prompted many commentators—led perhaps by James Luther Adams—to view them as *the* key to a vital, functioning democracy. Among other things, they take responsibility to represent the unrepresented (Ralph Nader and his consumer research organization); they hold private and public powers accountable to the rules of the game (American Civil Liberties Union); they sensitize the society to coming needs and problems that are not yet recognized (Zero Population Growth); they provide channels of participation in public life; and they have abilities to do things with humaneness that government or profit-making programs cannot do so well (hospitals, orphanages, homes for mentally retarded, etc.).

Not the least important of these intentional social units is the institutional church itself. No matter how debased or perverted, it is still the bearer of the Jewish and Christian story. Without the institutions to carry forward the classic symbols of the story, it would soon die of neglect or gradual warping. And the civil religion, noninstitutional as it seems to be, would lose its sustenance. Reinhold Niebuhr remarked that any achievement of justice deteriorates quickly if it is not constantly prodded to higher levels by a transcendent ideal. In like manner, the American myth will deteriorate to the Legionnaire's Creed quite quickly if it is not sustained by the more organized bearers of the symbols and myths.

The Cultural

Finally, there is the cultural context that limits and sustains, that gives a sense of belonging, and we cannot do justice to this sphere in this short chapter. Customs, values, persisting attitudes and character traits, common perspectives—in sum, the American ethos itself provides the substratum—the great, moving, mysterious stream—of belonging. One only knows the power of such persisting objective realities when one experiences "culture shock" in another land with alien traditions. For good or bad, they constitute the attitudinal foundations upon which the social and political are built. Obviously, the political and social spheres influence the cultural, but the limits and directions of politics and society are conditioned decisively by the underlying cultural continuities.

Our literary and cinematic artists are among the most sensitive portrayers of the American ethos. They are able to capture the "feel" of America better than sociologists or political analysts.

One thinks, for instance, of American writers who illuminate the life of a particular region. John Cheever writes of Yankees old and new who have been shaped by New England's land and culture. William Faulkner elicits the sights, sounds, smells, and feelings of the Deep South. John Updike makes Pennsylvania come alive for the reader. Urban environment and culture are reflected in the works of Mailer, Malamud, Bellow.

Or we could point to movies, at times taken from books, that evoke a sense of place, of locale. Westerns exploit the wide-open, rugged country of Colorado, Montana, etc. Movies like *The Last Picture Show, Five Easy Pieces,* and *In Cold Blood* are set in the flat, sparsely settled, desolate areas of Kansas, Oklahoma, or Texas. Suburban and urban settings of many movies capture the feel of living in American metropolises. *The Pawn Broker, The Graduate,* and *Save the Tiger* are some important examples.

At any rate, novels and movies attest to the substance of American culture—its feel for places and regions, its attitudes, values, customs, styles. Although many times faddish, novels and movies are the pulse of American life. When one reads or views the best of them, one can sense what it means to be an American, to belong to a particular culture.

Other distinctive traits of American culture—that give it form and substance—are its ethnic pluriformity, its open and informal life-style, its patterns of sports participation and observation, its diverse customs that surround the life-cycle—birth, marriage, and death, and its dance, music, and crafts indigenous to specific groups and places.

Our participation in these cultural realities brings a sense of belonging. These are the things one misses when one is absent from them. Their utter facticity hits home when people mistakenly think it is an easy matter to become an expatriate. Blacks who believe they have a great cultural affinity with Africans find out quickly that they are American. Very few of the military dropouts who went to Sweden remain there comfortably. Suffice it to say that American culture does have distinct substance. One can belong with vigor and appreciation. This is not to say the culture is an unmixed blessing. It is the bearer of the American myth; it is the matrix of the sustaining and limiting contexts. It is also the bearer of attitudes, values, and customs which work against the best in our heritage. Its commercialism, its crassness, its mindless activism are all too familiar. But let us begin at the beginning. Before anyone can be persuaded to change himself, he needs affirmation for what he is—both *because* of his gifts and potentialities and in *spite of* his shortcomings and hangups. It is no different with a nation.

NOTES

[1] R. W. B. Lewis, *The American Adam* (Chicago: The University of Chicago Press, 1955), p. 1.

[2] Robert Bellah, "Civil Religion in America," *Daedalus* (Winter 1967), p. 7.

[3] Ibid.

[4] Edward Johnson, *Wonder-Working Providence, 1628–1651*, ed. J. Franklin Jameson (New York: Charles Scribner's Sons, 1910), pp. 24–25. As cited by Nelvin Vos in "The American Dream Turned Nightmare: Recent American Drama," *Christian Scholars Review*, vol. I, no. 3 (Spring 1971), p. 195

[5] R. W. B. Lewis, *American Adam*, p. 3.

[6] Arend van Leeuwen, *Christianity and World History* (New York: Charles Scribner's Sons, 1964), pp. 158–184. See also Francis Fitzgerald, *Fire in the Lake* (New York: Vintage Books, 1972), chap. 1.

[7] R. W. Lewis, *American Adam*, p. 21.

[8] Daniel Boorstin, *The Americans: The National Experience* (New York: Vintage Books, 1967), p. 95.

[9] Eric Sevareid, "The American Dream" in *The Way It Is*, ed. Douglas Hughes (New York: Holt Rinehart & Winston, 1970), p. 50.

[10] Jean Jacques Servan-Schreiber, *The American Challenge*, trans. by Ronald Steel (New York: Atheneum, 1968), p. 6.

[11] R. W. Lewis, *American Adam*, p. 5.

[12] Daniel Boorstin, *Americans: National Experience*, pp. 34–44.

[13] Servan-Schreiber, *American Challenge*, p. 4.

[14] Daniel Boorstin, *Americans: National Experience*, p. 1.

[15] Eric Sevareid, *American Dream*, p. 51.

[16] Ibid.

[17] Gibson Winter, "The Question of Liberty in a Technologized World" in *A Creative Recovery of American Tradition*, ed. W. Taylor Stevenson *Anglican Theological Review*, Supplementary Series, no. 1 (July 1973), p. 8.

[18] Carl Becker, *Freedom and Responsibility in the American Way of Life* (New York: Vintage Books, 1955), p. 19.

[19] As cited in Hans Morgenthau, *The Purpose of American Politics* (New York: Alfred A. Knopf, 1969), p. 320.

[20] Ibid., p. 321.

[21] Walter Lippmann, in an interview in the Chicago *Sun-Times* on Sunday, March 25, 1973, sec. I-A, p. 12.

[22] H. Richard Niebuhr, *The Kingdom of God in America* (New York: Harper Torchbooks, 1957), p. 69.

[23] Ibid., p. 80.

[24] Ibid., p. 56.

[25] See above, note 2.

Chapter II

The Dark Side of the Myth

History shows that over and over again the achievements of
man, as though by a logic of tragedy, turn against man
himself.

Paul Tillich
The World Situation

CONTRAPUNTAL THEMES WITHIN THE VISION

From the very beginning of our history, there has been dissent
from the optimism of the American myth with its "sleek and
comely innocence." Lewis, for instance, points out that resistance to
Adamic innocence came from the Puritan tradition represented by
Jonathan Edwards and Horace Bushnell, and from the tragic vision
represented by novelists like Hawthorne and Melville. The dissent-
ers grappled with the darker realities of human life in the traditional Christian doctrines of the Fall, of original sin, and of the
ongoing presence of evil in man and the world.

For these writers there could be no completely new beginning in
human history. There could be no human nature unpolluted by the
Fall of Adam. Evil was not external to man, as was implied by the
notion that the American stood free of the corrupting civilizations
of Europe and was thereby innocent and new.

Indeed, for them the human freedom lifted up by the predominant myth was highly ambiguous. The limits of the past could be
the groundwork of civilized society; leaving them might mean a
degeneration into barbarity. The soaring ascent could be used for
evil purposes as well as good. The future that met the ascent might
unexpectedly strike down that quest. Nature had within it the
capacity for evil and death as well as life. Consistent with the
Christian tradition, these writers argued that, while nature and
human spirit were good, they were corruptible. In fact, in the reality of life on earth they were inextricably mixed—all that is good
is corrupted and all that is evil is corrupted good.

Hawthorne and Melville wrote, Lewis argues, from a more profound Christian vision that had a deeper grasp of the relation between good and evil, life and death. Hawthorne was aware that:

> Beneath the sunshine that illuminates the soul's surface, there is a region of horror that seems, to the inward traveler, like hell itself, and through which the self wanders without hope; but deeper still there is a place of perfect beauty. . . . There is possible some fulfillment of spirit, some realization of the entire self which it was worth losing one's self to find; only the lost, indeed, were likely to find it on their return journey, though a soul might shrivel in the process.[1]

Perhaps this is getting too close to a Christian vision of redemption to be relevant to the shaping of a national myth. One could not expect that such a deep and ambiguous view of man's story could become the basis of a national myth. But there is no doubt that such a vision is utterly important in the *chastening* of such myths. It can open us to dimensions of the human spirit that we neglect at our peril. In this chastening function the Christian symbols find a proper role. But this subject will be treated at length later.

Melville, influenced by Hawthorne, also saw the darkness that Hawthorne's "truth-telling" revealed beneath the superficial appearances of the world. His book, *Moby Dick*, probes evil in the world; the White Whale is itself the symbol of an evil force in nature unrecognized in the optimistic philosophies of Emerson and Thoreau. It also probes the ambiguity of the human spirit, tempted and led by evil as well as good. *Moby Dick* is both a drama and a parable in which the hero, Ahab, follows his genius to the extremes recommended by Emerson and Thoreau. He ascends in free flight. But Ahab reveals to the reader that he, like his biblical prototype, is led by a "lying spirit" to a bad end. Melville himself betrays a fascination with the monomania that infected Ahab. It is this sympathy—this feeling that "there but for the grace of God go I"—toward a hero with a tragic flaw that makes Moby Dick a book to brood over. It possesses the ambiguity of all great tragedy because its hero fails in the midst of a struggle in which good and evil are no longer clear-cut.

This kind of sensitivity to evil decisively qualifies the American myth. Abraham Lincoln, whom some have called the greatest American theologian of the nineteenth century, possessed deep insight into the ambiguity of human affairs. In his magnificent second inaugural address he powerfully illuminates our relative view of God's will, a view tainted by our own interests. At the same time he stands humbly before the mystery of God's judgment and grace.

> Both read the same Bible and pray to the same God, and each invokes His aid against the other. . . . The prayers of both could not be answered. That of neither has been answered fully. The Almighty has His own purposes. "Woe unto the world because of offenses, for it must needs be that offenses come, but woe to that man by whom the offense cometh." . . . Fondly do we hope, fervently do we pray, that this mighty scourge of war may speedily pass away. Yet, if God wills that it continue until all the wealth piled by the bondman's two hundred and fifty years of unrequited toil shall be sunk, and until every drop of blood drawn with the lash shall be paid by another drawn with the sword, as was said three thousand years ago, so still it must be said, "The judgments of the Lord are true and righteous altogether."
>
> With malice toward none, with charity for all, with firmness in the right as God gives us to see the right, let us strive on to finish the work we are in, to bind up the nation's wounds; to care for him who shall have borne the battle, and for his widow and his orphans, to do all which may achieve and cherish a just and a lasting peace among ourselves and with all nations.

Examples like this—from writers of fiction and from a President grounded in biblical wisdom—provide contrapuntal themes that qualify the optimism of the American Adamic myth. They challenge the notion of innocence by pointing up the pervasive and tragic self-interest involved in all human projects. They bear witness to the fact that the soaring ascents of individuals and groups are made at the expense and pain of others, and that they frequently come to a bad end. Judgment falls upon flawed human character as it struggles upward in strife with others. Life has a measure of that "war of all against all" that the pessimists of every age describe.

But such wisdom is not the grist for modern national myths. And the realists about human nature could not win the American attention. The Adamic myth won out and the version of the American dream elaborated above became the driving story for the culture.

As we proceed along the literary tradition, we find continuing celebrations of the myth in such varied writers as James Fenimore Cooper, Ralph Waldo Emerson, Henry David Thoreau, Henry Wadsworth Longfellow, Oliver Wendell Holmes, and, above all, Walt Whitman, the "poet of democracy." The basic structure of the myth—shaking free of the past, the ascending struggle in the present, met by a gracious open future—was affirmed and communicated.

However, except for a few notable exceptions—Carl Sandburg, Thomas Wolfe, and the early Saul Bellow—the great stream of the literary tradition seems to have changed directions. Instead of undergirding and reinforcing the naive dynamism and innocence of the American dream, literature from the post-Civil War period onward dwells on the dark side of the myth. In fact, instead of seeing the myth as ambiguous—with its bright and optimistic side mixed with its dark and ominous side—most of the major writers from the late nineteenth century to the present interpret the myth not as the American dream, but rather as the American nightmare. Theodore Dreiser, Upton Sinclair, Irving Babbitt, Sinclair Lewis, and John Dos Passos wrote during a period of rising industrialism. They were attuned to the hollowness of the dream for those individuals and groups of people who were exploited or crushed by the triumphant ascent of corporate power. They witnessed to the nightmarish existence of the little people whose ascent was blocked by the concentrated power of monopolies that were by that time reinforced by a growing technology.

At any rate, two significant assumptions of the American myth were being challenged: first, that the ascent of groups struggling upward was fundamentally innocent; and second, that open geographical and social space was virtually limitless. It was becoming clear in an industrial age that corporate self-interest was not mitigated by natural (morally innocent) self-limits. Indeed, the questing spirit that creatively built the industrial empires also pushed through them toward ever-increasing profits and power. Moreover, in earlier days before the onslaught of industrialism, the ascent of powerful groups had wide-open social and geographical spaces in which to thrust their projects. But with the growth of an industrial mode of social relations, the expansion of the cities. the influx of millions of new immigrants, and the narrowing of the frontier, these corporate ascents could not rise without exploiting the land and its resources and without crushing or manipulating the people caught in their draft. The writers of that era of developing industrialism were sensitive to these events and sharply challenged the optimism of the myth.

An instructive response to developing industrialism was that of the southern literary tradition. Southern writers argued from a perspective that never did participate fully in the American dream. The South, dominated by a landed aristocracy, static social classes and castes, a homogeneous population on either side of the dividing line between blacks and whites, heavy social and religious tradition, and a mentality of isolation, kept itself free of the dynamism of the American dream and practice.[2] After reconstruction and amid the ensuing industrialization of the rest of the country, southern literature self-consciously created an alternative to the American dream. It culminated in the twelve southern authors who brought out *I'll Take My Stand* in 1930. Here they outlined their program of old-fashioned pastoral agrarianism. They were, so to say, looking hopefully backward.

But this option was challenged by the writings of William Faulkner, himself a Southerner with impeccable credentials. In his works, the static, hallowed traditions of the South decay from within. The aristocratic heritage moves inexorably into blind alleys and tragic ends. The land and sons are lost. White trash—symbolized by the Snopes family—takes over. Immersed in this fateful decline, Negroes suffer vicariously on behalf of all.

If the southern option leads to Faulkner's *Götterdämmerung*, the northern option fares no better in its own artistic tradition. Nelvin Vos, whose essay, "The American Dream Turned to Nightmare; Recent American Drama," is seminal for this present study, has analyzed the movement from dream to nightmare in recent American drama. Eugene O'Neill, America's most distinguished playwright, is prototypical of this movement. His first play, *Bound East for Cardiff* (1916), illustrates his early affirmation of the dream. The main character has a dream of leaving his poverty-stricken home and moving to America where he can reach for the promise of a home of his own and children to sustain his name. The character's name is Yank![3]

Later on O'Neill transposed that dream to something quite different. In *Desire Under the Elms* (1924) and *Long Day's Journey into Night* (1941), O'Neill reveals "that the society whose imperfection he exposed was still wasting itself, as he once said, in 'that everlasting game of trying to possess your own soul by the possession of something outside it.' "[4] In both plays archetypal Yankee patriarchs lose their hopes for the continuing possession and enrichment of their land by their sons. The sons turn bad in both cases and the Abrahamic promise of land and sons is lost. The dream turns into a nightmare.

Arthur Miller bears forward the same themes in *All My Sons* (1947) and *Death of a Salesman* (1949). Vos writes concerning the former play:

> Joe Keller, factory owner, is more interested in personal aggrandizement and society's favor than he is in responsibility for others. The exposé of his personal failure to reject faulty aircraft parts leads to the older son's decision to commit suicide and the younger son's repudiation of his father. Miller portrays Joe Keller not as villainous but as weak. Keller bows under pressure; he is indecisive. When Keller is aware that he is responsible for his own actions, that others, as he says just before the end of the play, are "all my sons," he kills himself. ... In the father's final act of self-destruction, his decisiveness is an attempt to gain his dignity once more. But the dream of a rosy future with wealth and heirs has been shattered.[5]

The plot of *Death of a Salesman* is familiar to most. Willy Loman is the archetype of the American salesman, soaring up from nowhere to reach his dreams. But his sons are ne'er-do-wells. His hopes for a "place in the country" fall apart with the lives of his sons. Overshadowing his failures are the grand American successes of his brother, Ben, who possesses both sons (seven of them!) and land in Alaska. Ben is crass, ruthless, and successful: "Why, boys, when I was seventeen I walked into the jungle, and when I was twenty-one I walked out. (He laughs) And by God I was rich."

The Dream therefore is fulfilled for some, but Willy's version of the dream, according to Biff [his son], was phony. When Willy is convinced that Biff still loves him, he destroys himself to give his sons the $20,000 from his insurance. He dies for his dream; for his sons and money, but Charley [his friend and neighbor] perceptively comments at the graveside that Willy "had all the wrong dreams." . . . Biff has gained in self-knowledge at the end of the action, but for Willy, there is little, if any, awareness of his illusions. Just as the setting of the play is described as "a dream arising out of reality," so Willy's early musings lead to the crescendo nightmare of suicide. Willy has sold himself for a mess of pottage, for when Miller was asked what Willy was selling, what was in his bags, the author's only reply was "Himself."[6]

With uncanny precision, Vos goes on to show how the most significant plays of Tennessee Williams and Edward Albee are obsessed with the same motifs. Only in the more recent plays, rather than the hope for land, the hope for healthy and robust sons seems to be the one dashed in nightmarish tragedies.

As Vos concludes:

The value of time is certainly one of the main differences between the people of the dream and the people of the nightmare. In the dream, the past is renounced, the present enjoyed, and therefore the future is open and pregnant with possibilities. To possess land and wealth as well as a male heir is to continue one's name and to be assured of immortality, if not in heaven, at least in the cherished memory of others. In the nightmare, one is haunted by the past. This leads to uncertainty and despair in the present, and therefore the future, if it exists at all, is ominous and foreboding. Time and history become a burden.[7]

Thus, early writers like Hawthorne and Melville saw the presence of evil below the surface of every human appearance. Later writers perceived the rampant and destructive self-interest in corporate ascent. In the later dramatists we have just examined, however, the problem does not center on strong-willed, greedy, or power-hungry villains. The problem centers on the decay of potency, of human vigor, in the fathers and sons. A degeneration of the willing spirit has taken place. The moral freshness, newness, and initiative of the original Adam is lost. Spines melt. The hoped-for future is forfeited by a wilting of character. The dream can be lost by moral stagnation as well as aggressive evil intentions.

In the writing of very recent American novelists, another but complementary theme seems to crop up. The dream is not shattered by strong-willed egomaniacs—be they individual or corporate. Nor is it destroyed by the moral laxness of the characters. Rather, it seems that the characters are willing to leave the limits of their past and struggle upward toward their hopes. But it is the character of the future itself that dashes them down. Instead of the American future being open and gracious, it is dense, threatening, crowded, and confused. In short, it is the enemy of human effort toward self-realization.

In his early career, Saul Bellow wrote his *Adventures of Augie March* and *Henderson the Rain King* in which strong, eccentric, and colorful American characters plunge vigorously into a challenging and fascinating future. Later, his stories take quite a different shape. The main characters of *Dangling Man, Herzog,* and *Mr. Sammler's Planet* are all caught in an urban environment in which complexities, confusions, and overt dangers thwart their lives.

Updike's Piet, in *Couples,* is not bothered by lack of potency or human vigor. He is placed in a suburban environment that finally frustrates him by its sterile, robot-like men and frustrated women. The social landscape closes in on him. At the end of *Rabbit, Run,* Harry Angstrom is running down a nameless highway to nowhere. In the sequel, *Rabbit Redivivus,* Harry's modest hopes of home and family are nearly destroyed by enveloping drug problems, runaway children, hostile blacks, and general societal indifference. Harry, who began his young life with hopes high, resigns himself to the cluttered and puzzling American environment.

Perhaps Ken Kesey's *One Flew Over the Cuckoo's Nest* most sharply illustrates the loss of a gracious, open American future. The archetypal Irish-American, MacMurphy, is finally crushed by the Combine, the term Kesey uses for the gigantic social and political conspiracy he believes wants to train and regiment us all. Certainly, MacMurphy is the American Adam in entirety. He has shaken the limits of his past; he has struggled vigorously with the world. But the future is closed, ordered, tightly controlled. It will not allow spontaneous, free flights. The landscape—social and geographical—is laid out like a printed electrical circuit. And humans must fit in. Liberty is gone. The American dream becomes a nightmare again.

What are we to make of this startling reversal in which celebration of the American dream turns to repeated scenes of nightmare? It seems that what once was a minor undercurrent in a vast sea of optimism in our literary tradition has now emerged as a sweeping flood.

It could be—as some of our positive thinkers have charged—that artists are simply more alienated from the American dream and reality than the majority of American people. Aren't artists always on the outside, looking in? But that doesn't account for the earlier American tradition in which artists were the prime movers in extolling the American dream. Weren't they just as much on the outside then?

Perhaps one can even have a more cynical view. Artists have to make a big splash in American highbrow circles if they are to survive—an even bigger splash if they are to become famous. Therefore, they are driven to exploit the most bizarre and horrendous aspects of American life. They must leap atop the latest fad and exaggerate it even further. Radical politics, explicit sex, and violence have had their turn as favorite subjects. But this of course does not account for those numerous serious artists who shun publicity and are already established.

Another interpretation takes the heat off the artist. Perhaps it isn't the artist that is at fault; it could be that the American dream itself is intrinsically demonic. Artists are simply the first to see that and report it. As it was said about Willy Loman at his funeral, "His dreams were all wrong." However, that very line was said by Willy's next-door neighbor whose son had pursued the American dream also, become a respected professional, and had presented him with grandchildren.

While each of these interpretations may have some measure of truth to them, they scarcely do justice either to the artist or to the complexity of the American dream and reality. A more adequate perspective might consider that from the beginning the artistic tradition has had contrapuntal themes within it sensitive to the ambiguity of the American myth. The myth was seen as gigantic cumulus clouds whose topside soared in glorious ascending contours into the shining sun. But like those same clouds, there were dark, churning storms on the underside. We were never so innocent as we thought we were—we have always left human wreckage in our past. Our struggling ascents were never so potent and inexorable as' we thought; there were always pathetic and tragic people whose ascents were destroyed by one flaw or another. There were always people, like Uncle Ben, whose ascent was not characterized by exhilarating achievement that had benefits for all but rather by greedy will-to-power that meant diminishing others. The future was never so automatically open and gracious as we thought. Even the brightest and best ascents have at unexpected times been met by future's tragic fate.

In a mature technological society, innocence, unwavering ascent, and a reliably beneficent future are no longer plausible. And our artists have pointed that out. It is not that the American dream is wholly demonic. It is rather that it is blind to its own underside. The structure of existence itself makes an unchastened American dream incredible and impossible.

Our people—like all people—have experienced evil flaws, and quirks of fate. But their deeper vision has been averted by an optimistic myth that skips from one bright peak to another. Our artists are now giving their interpretation of experiences of evil that are basic to everyone. What was tragic about Willy Loman was that his experience of evil, fault, and fate did not chasten his dreams. He thought his ascent could be steeper and farther than the possibilities given him. His illusions kept him from coming to terms with his real situation. And the illusory dreams degenerated into a nightmare.

We would propose that what our artists are about is such a chastening of our dreams. Novelists and poets are revealing the dark underside—sometimes in exaggerated form. They are interpreting our experience of the underside as a concomitant effect of the pretension of the dream itself.

Whether or not the artistic tradition has deeply affected the American common consciousness, it is clear that recent events have. Indeed, we believe that the decade of the sixties has decisively revealed the ambiguity of the American myth and reality. Events of nationwide significance constantly bombarded the American consciousness in that period. In those events, the evil spin-offs of the myth became clear in real history. We turn now to that new consciousness of ambiguity mediated through recent events.

THE REVELATION OF FORGOTTEN REALITIES

The prior victory of the Adamic myth has made Americans peculiarly blind to its destructive spin-offs. This blindness is partly due to the fact that there is so much objective evidence that corroborates the basic, but partial, truth of the myth. Americans by and large have done well. There has been an upward ascent and the land has been sweet and good. We've reached the moon.

However, in the Christian tradition the most dangerous heresies have been rooted in partial truths which claim to be the whole truth. So it is with successful national myths. Their success claims to be total. Evil is always corrupted or exaggerated good. The most monstrous evils are generated out of movements that at one point appear to be idealistic and healthy. As Reinhold Niebuhr has asserted, the potentialities for evil grow with the potentialities for good. History cumulates rather than solves the deepest dilemmas of humankind. America is no exception to this basic truth. Because we have lifted up the creativity and dynamic of the free, unfettered spirit with such success (the potentialities for good), we have been peculiarly blind to the problems inherent in such a cultural myth (the potentialities for evil). Thus, as we have moved forward in history with increasing size and power, we cumulate the goods and evils on both sides of the ledger. So we are at once the best and worst of nations. Moreover, these extremes are only possible because we have latched onto a profound human good. But whereas we have been attuned to the heights of the human spirit, we have been blind to its depths.

A word here is appropriate regarding the role of technology in pointing up the ambiguities of the American myth. In contrast with many commentators—Ellul, Roszak, Reich among others— who tend to view technology as inherently destructive of human good, we perceive technology as the magnified extension of human capacities. As such it only accentuates the human intentions—good, evil, or mixed—behind it; it does not add a new direction on its own. But because of this magnification, the possibilities and problems of every effort are blown up to gigantic proportions. And because technology relentlessly pursues the ends it was created to accomplish, it needs continual redirection and monitoring by its human overseers, or else it destroys its creator.

The decade of the sixties was marked by the explosive emergence of long-smoldering problems. We saw the racial problem surface in the civil rights movement and then the Black Power movement. We saw the development of the Indian movement for self-determination. We experienced the blossoming of ecological concern on a massive scale. Related problems of overpopulation, poor nutrition, and overall health care came with it or anticipated it. Ralph Nader's coordinated efforts began to deal with abuses of the consumer. The peace movement reached its zenith even as the war in Indochina achieved a crescendo pitch. Student dissent and rebelliousness were fanned not only by the war but also by movements toward decentralization and "participatory democracy." Urban decay and transition became more evident in the sixties than ever before. The women's liberation movement emerged with jarring and persisting power. Concern for the elderly grew. The drug problem reached its highpoint on both military and civilian fronts. Inflation increased and our balance of payments began to totter.

When that list of problems is enumerated, one wonders how we survived. One also begins to understand why we elected a President who promised to bank the fires of change.

In the following we hope to outline the close and complex relation of possibilities to problems. In order to indicate the ambiguity of the matter—the close relation of good to evil—we will correlate each serious challenge with the strengths of the myth we have already examined. In this way, the dark underside of the shining myth becomes evident.

"To Shake Free of the Limiting Past . . ."

In the American rush from the past to the future, in our social and geographical mobility, we have left vast amounts of wreckage in our pasts. It has become clear that we cannot innocently move from one frontier to the next without leaving many wounded behind.

Perhaps the Indian tribes—hunting people caught in an onrush of agricultural and industrial development—have the dubious honor of being the first wreckage of the American myth. We slaughtered them first, then tucked away those left on isolated reservations and forgot them. Black people provide another instance of wreckage left behind. At one time economically necessary in the South, blacks were left in a crippled state as the wreckage of a developing agricultural and industrial system. The cities are another example of wreckage. Use them and move on, forgetting any adequate responsibility to what is left. After waves upon waves of the world's poor immigrants have moved through our center cities—and continue to move through for that matter—the cities are tired and depleted. But our society forgets. Senior citizens caught in declining cities and rural areas are passed by in a youth-oriented, onward-rushing society. In our misguided war in Indochina, we have probably wrecked several societies for generations as we struggled upward to "help our friends."

Of course the most obvious and frightening instance of wreckage in the past relates to the ecological problem. In our expanding consumer society we thought we could continue pushing forward with increasing production and consumption without having nature catch up with us. But the waste we leave behind us won't go away. It clutters the landscape, contaminates the water and food, and pollutes the air. Because of our assumption of limitless space we thought we could spew out all the refuse behind us. But space— even American space—is not limitless. The wreckage left behind encompasses us.

Less obvious but perhaps just as threatening is our tendency to use our sustaining contexts, our structures of belonging from which we emerged and were given identity, as mere launching pads for our ascent into the future. These structures of belonging are then cast off behind us, much as the first stages of long-range rockets are left behind in a moon shot. They are not cared for or preserved, for there is no looking back. The "place" from which we came, the people, the groups, the institutions, the friendships are left behind to fend for themselves as we press forward with our social and geographical mobility. The launching pads are left to rust and no new ones are found.

Melvin Webber, describing the emergence of the "cosmopolite" in a "post-city age," asserts somewhat enthusiastically that a sense of "place" is a thing of the past. Spatially located people are simply those who have not kept up with the truly mobile society.

> By now, the large metropolitan centers that used to be primarily goods-producing foci have become interchange junctions within the international communications networks. Only in the limited geographical, physical sense is any modern metropolis a discrete, unitary, identifiable phenomenon. At most, it is a localized node within the integrating international networks, finding its significant identity as contributor to the workings of that larger system. As a result, the new cosmopolites belong to none of the world's metropolitan areas, although they use them.[8]

The life of the cosmopolite is a correlate of this new "status" of the city. He dwells nowhere. Webber used an example of an academic astronomer, "based" at a major university:

> But the striking thing about our astronomer, and the millions of people like him engaged in other professions, is how little of his attention and energy he devotes to the concerns of the place-defined communities. Surely, as compared to his grandfather, whose life was largely bound up in the affairs of his locality, the astronomer, playwright, newsman, steel broker, or wheat dealer lives in a life-space that is not defined by territory and deals with problems that are not local in nature. For him, the city is but a convenient setting for the conduct of his professional work; it is not the basis for the social communities that he cares most about.[9]

Those who have not been mobile enough to make it into the post-city age are left to care for the launching pad. It is not difficult to see why our cities have dim futures. But perhaps we will stop short of the time when Webber claims that the

> ... meaning of "community" will be archaic and disappear from common usage. It has already lost much of its traditional meaning for a great many of those on the leading edge of society. If it is retained, it may be restricted to the provisions of children and of those adults who have not gained access to modern society.[10]

The proper mixture of horror and exhilaration one has in reading the above simply corresponds with the ambiguity of the American myth itself. By soaring above and away from structured space,
we may find ourselves floating in unstructured space with no sense
of belonging, no moorings at all.

Vos captures the ominous effects of this free floating mobility.

> Not only time, but also space is a dimension of the dream and the
> nightmare. To be rooted in, and to have one's offspring become
> heirs to, a particular piece of land is to provide much more than
> real estate and security. Such space gives meaning; it may even, in
> Mircea Eliade's term, be transformed into a sacred place, an *axis
> mundi*, that is, the center of the world, the navel of the earth, that
> out of which one's identity is born. But in the versions of the
> nightmare we have explored, the meaning of space has been
> destroyed. All space is the same which neutralizes the significance
> of space and erodes the meaningfulness of particular places. Con-
> temporary mobility is not, strictly speaking, a movement to places.
> Instead, as Tom Driver has pointed out, mobility is "movement to
> where certain people happen to live, to where they gather, to cer-
> tain equipment (people plus equipment equal the office) or where
> certain events are scheduled." Such mobility provides the illusion
> of freedom but, without an *axis mundi*, the feeling is one of aliena-
> tion and lostness.[11]

This tendency to abandon the wreckage of the past—be it structured space, Indians, blacks, used consumer products, urban areas,
etc.—is endemic to the American myth. It is the dark side of the
injunction to shake free of the limits of the past. But the last
decade has shown us that we can no longer innocently—if we ever
could—plunge forward into the future without taking responsibility for the charred and rusted hulks we have left behind us. The
task ahead of us is a difficult one: how do we maintain the
dynamic acceleration and exhilaration of the American dream and
yet take responsibility for the past left behind?

"In a Struggling Ascent . . ."

If our myth's accentuation of freedom from the past produces
some serious challenges, its lifting up of initiative as a key element
presents corresponding difficulties. What of those members of our
society who cannot or will not ascend, who cannot or will not par-

ticipate in the competitive struggle to achieve socially approved goals?

The decade of the sixties revealed to us the existence of large minorities mired in a "culture of poverty" that created internal restraints in their members. Michael Harrington, in his *The Other America*, and Oscar Lewis, in *La Vida*, documented the presence and persistence of such groups among ghetto-dwelling blacks and Latins and among white hill people who remain in their rural pockets of poverty or who migrate to urban centers.

Edward Banfield characterizes the culture of poverty as a "lower-class" time orientation. While the upper class, middle class, and working class have a future dimension built into the pattern of their lives, the lower class is almost exclusively present oriented. By lower class Banfield does not mean simply meager economic income. Indeed, many poor people have a working-class or middle-class time orientation and they are the ones that tend to become mobile. They have a real chance of throwing off the limits of the past and struggling upward. But the "lower-class" orientation lives for the present. Not enough planning, not enough deferred pleasure, not enough education, not enough saving or investment—in short, not enough disciplined initiative dooms the lower-class culture of poverty to the life of hustling in the streets. When this time orientation gets ensconced in an ongoing family pattern, it is passed down from generation to generation.[12]

A persisting culture of poverty is stubbornly resistant to any kind of quick transformation, but it is doubly difficult for Americans. First, we find it hard to believe that people are not *naturally* ambitious. Doesn't everyone want to better himself in ways that are acceptable to the whole society? If people don't understand the kind of social and cultural conditioning going on in a culture of poverty, they, in much more ominous fashion, tend to attribute the lack of ambition to something inherent in racial or biological characteristics. Then they believe the condition of the culture of poverty to be permanent.

Our libertarian tradition hampers us in our efforts to deal with cultures of poverty. And rightly so. We have no tradition that would enable the state to intervene decisively in the lives of disorganized families. Compulsory birth control, compulsory pre-school-ing, and intentional educational isolation of children from parents are all *verboten* in our society. Semi-military work camps for hustlers are likewise taboo. Since no one has invented some other quick solution to this problem, we tend to wait and hate. Our myth prevents both decisive intervention and permissive treatment. We now know about the phenomenon—who can be unaware of the relation of crime and drugs?—but we're not sure what to do about it.

A related problem before which our myth seems incompetent concerns the persistence of people whose native gifts are such that they cannot rise very high on the ladder of achievement. Our myth doesn't affirm people who cannot be more than waiters, garbage collectors, bus drivers, and common laborers. Besides living for their children's ascent, they have little that gives them significant affirmation in their own present. In Japan common laborers can work for the glory of the company and the national pride of Japan; in Russia bus drivers can participate in building socialism; in older European cultures waiters have pride in their work because it is honored by hoary tradition. Cultures with collectivist myths or older cultures with ontic traditions—in which every office in life has its perennial place in the nature of things—have ways of affirming the most menial of tasks. But the American myth rarely has such collectivist legitimations and never any ontic affirmations. Only in totally mobilized situations—World War II was perhaps the last instance—are all jobs given meaning because they are a part of the whole American effort.

Certainly another reality that we have become aware of in recent years are the blockages to ascent caused by external conditions. The sixties were a revelation of unemployment and underemployment caused by technological development. Increasing automation lopped off many low-skilled jobs that were once real channels of mobility upward. As the technology of production became more sophisticated, manufacturing concerns left their inner-city habitats —with their heavy, ponderous industrial base—for the suburbs where new technology made the production process cleaner and more streamlined. This left working-class populations in central-city areas without jobs. These external blockages to ascent were real and we became aware of them.

Nevertheless, if Americans are Americans, the majority tend to have expectations of ascent or at least expectations of the benefits of ascent. The myth elevates the expectations but cannot guarantee their realization. When the expectations are frustrated, bitterness is a direct consequence.

If our cultural story makes it difficult to understand and deal with people who *cannot* ascend, it stands absolutely helpless before people who *will* not. A minority—increasing now—neither wants to achieve socially sanctioned goals nor does it expect the benefits of the achievement. Dropouts, who merely want to "be," and not achieve, must find very isolated nooks and crannies in order to exist free of contempt and harassment. An activist myth cannot tolerate this kind of "uselessness." A related difficulty concerns an American inability to enjoy quiet and passive forms of leisure. Leisure time tends to be filled with frenetic activity that does not complement the achievement pole of life, but rather is merely an extension of that very thing.

Again, as with the first moment of the American myth, the second moment—to move upward in struggling ascent—has a dark side. Its activism and voluntarism has little patience for or comprehension of immobilized people or for more passive modes of life. It maximizes liberty, initiative, and creativity but has defective ways of dealing with basic security and creating a corporate morale which can compensate for individual failure or rejection of ascent.

"Toward the Realization of Promise in a Gracious, Open Future"

The final moment in the American myth has assumed limitless social and geographical space. And that space has been understood as basically hospitable, gracious to the ascent from the limits of the past. Here again the objective facts of the past have been undeniable. For many, perhaps the overwhelming majority, doors have opened in American society. The reality of the gracious future has corresponded to the myth. Social and geographical horizons have been open, graciously receiving the projects laid upon them.

But the spaces have been closing. Partly due to the very success of the ascents coming from the past and partly due to the magnification of those ascents by a rapidly developing technology, we have become a mature industrial nation with a closely knit, interdependent social and economic fabric. But in the past we have not acknowledged that interdependence.

This is not to say that the future is completely closed. But it is to say that it is increasingly difficult to find the interstices in a rather cluttered and competitive scene. A dimension of this problem turns on the rate of speed at which the future comes at us. The future is not only cluttered, competitive, and complex, it is also moving toward us so fast that it becomes increasingly difficult to find one's way in the onrushing maze. The openings appear for a moment and are gone. As Toffler pointed out in *Future Shock,* a very likely response to this onrush is bewilderment, retreat, and withdrawal. (Incidentally, the symbol of our awareness of this onrushing and cluttering of the future is the phenomenal sales of Toffler's book.)

The dark side of this moment in our dramatic myth is that we were lulled into believing that our social and geographical landscape was infinite, limitless. Therefore, the future would always be open and gracious. Illusions of infinity, like illusions that we could innocently abandon the past and that all people were self-starters, can continue to blind us to the ambiguity of the myth. The shining topside grasps and fosters a profound truth about human life. But that truth is not complete, not sufficient. If allowed to push forward unchecked—if the dark side is not attended to—it could spell our demise.

Some Conventional Unhelpful Responses

Whenever a society is confronted with the concentration of social eruptions that occurred in America in the sixties, typical responses are sharpened. Classic stances toward societal challenges are etched more clearly than in quiescent times. And so we have responses from the left, right, and middle. It is true that those traditional political categories are sometimes irrelevant today. So we will try to spell them out more clearly.

The *left* is the party of dissent. When it reaches the extremities of its tether, it is the party of despair. Then it has come full circle and shares many characteristics of its brothers on the right. The varieties of leftist dissent share a common approach in three ways.

First, they tend to see things as a whole system that is pervasively evil. They take little time to reflect on mixed blessings and curses. Pragmatic approaches to specific problems are anathema. The whole system must be destroyed and replaced by a new one.

The counter-cultural left sees the system as the repressive corporate state. Theodore Roszak refers to it as "science-based-urban-industrialism."[13] And the system is evil. Since America is the leader of "developed states" it is the most dangerous. One cannot transform or improve it by bits and pieces. A whole new cultural mindscape must emerge which will lead to a system far different from the horrendous one we have now.

Those segments of the left influenced by older Marxist ideas view the capitalist system as unambiguously evil. James Foreman's manifesto says it clearly:

> The people must be educated to understand that any black man or Negro who is advocating a perpetuation of capitalism inside the United States is in fact seeking not only his ultimate destruction and death but is contributing to the continuous exploitation of black people all around the world. For it is the power of the United States government, this racist, imperialist government, that is choking the life of all people around the world.[14]

Secondly, the evil system is based on a rather clearly definable external cause. The evil is not in human nature itself but in something we can destroy or eradicate. Roszak locates the evil cause in the scientific mindscape—single vision. Single vision flattens everything out to cause and effect, thereby destroying the sacramental depth present in all reality. If we could destroy the tyranny of "objective consciousness," the system would wither and die. Foreman places the cause—an obvious departure from Marxism—in white racism, which is what is actually behind capitalism. The western world (capitalism) was built on racism, not vice versa. If white racism can be smashed, capitalism will come tumbling down and the world will be rid of evil.

Thirdly, the despairing left comes forth with prescriptions that can only be termed delusions. The prescriptions are so far from the possibilities of the American scene that they boggle the mind. They are oblivious not only to the practical possibilities, but also to their own obvious flaws and dangers. Roszak would have science become magical and rhapsodic. We would not intervene in nature nor strive to achieve. Rather, we would bask in the religious transcendence of the visionary commonwealth.

Foreman's proposal is not so peaceful:

> Racism in the United States is so pervasive in the mentality of whites that only an armed, well-disciplined, black-controlled government can insure the stamping out of racism in this country. . . . We say . . . think in terms of total control of the United States. Prepare ourselves to seize state power.[15]

This is not to say that the counter-cultural and Marxist left are not responding to real problems. Roszak's book is a vigorous indictment of crass scientism. Foreman is angrily reacting to the effects of centuries of oppression. But neither strand is particularly helpful in balanced analysis of conditions and their causes, and certainly not helpful in constructive proposals.

The *right* is the party of assent. When it reaches the extremities of its tether, it is the party of suppression. Then it contradicts the very myth it intends to protect. The right in America continues to be drawn from the military-industrial complex. It also comes from people who are threatened by leftists telling them in speech and action that everything is wrong in America. Often these people gave all they had to be faithful to the American dream and don't want to see their lifetime efforts negated.

The right is characterized by its refusal to see the dark side of the American myth and reality. It pretends that we are what we are not. It has illusions and thus tends toward hypocrisy. The right has few boisterous propagandists, for rightists tend to have positions of power and need not resort to arguing with the dissidents.

The illusions of the right are being played out by the current administration. The wraps are being taken off the large, private corporate impulses while the government is withdrawing from the concerns of the public sphere. Social welfare and improvement programs are being liquidated. The illusion is that the future is open and gracious for all; if people really want to work they will make it.

The prescriptions of the right revolve about efforts to weaken some of the limiting contexts that have been constructed to check private power. If corporate ascent can be unfettered, our problems will be solved. How this deals with the wreckage of our past, the inability of some people to compete, and the cluttering of our future is anyone's guess.

The *center* is the party of balance. When it presses the principle of balance too far, it reaches the state of paralysis. This center encompasses the great majority of Americans. They may be left of center and are called liberals or Democrats. They may be somewhat right of center and are called conservatives or progressive Republicans. But they swing back and forth rather easily. The center is levelheaded; it is aware of the bright and dark sides of American myth and reality.

However, while it is aware of the ambiguity of American society, it tends to believe that by continuing checks and balances we can muddle through. If each competing interest (the center has a realistic notion of human motivation) is limited by another, a proper harmony will ensue. Unfortunately, the center has difficulty dealing with any notion of the *common* good. It assumes that the balancing of interests leads to the common good. But this is just another version of the invisible hand—that some providential force operates for the common good when interests are balanced. Without negating the notion of checks and balances, we would propose that we must move beyond harmony of interests to a notion of the common good if we are to avoid the peculiar sickness of the center, paralysis. Balancing competing groups will not deal adequately with the wreckage left in our past, with the persisting presence of people who cannot or will not participate in competitive ascent, or with the cluttering and closing of our future. Indeed, the mere balancing of competing interest, or the further inclusion of left-out groups, could just as well exacerbate the problems generated on the underside of the myth.

John C. Raines, in a critique of Reinhold Niebuhr's political thought, makes this same point:

> Indeed, the criticism of American interest group liberalism began precisely at a practical and everyday level and only later deepened into a theoretical criticism, including, if this essay is correct, a critique of its "heavenly justifications." Thus, people like John Kenneth Galbraith began to notice the curious irony of public poverty

in the midst of private wealth (*The Affluent Society*). Robert Paul Wolff (*The Poverty of Liberalism*) showed that the inner logic of the interest-group view of society, in its function of providing an interpretive floor for relatively stable political calculations, depended upon everyone and every group "acting selfishly," with no place for the recognition of the common good. Finally, people like Edelman (*The Symbolic Uses of Politics*), Lowi (*The End of Liberalism*), and Schattschneider (*The Semi-sovereign People*) pointed out that American politics had, indeed, no way of handling the politics of the common good because it was so fundamentally a policy of organized interest-group trade-offs.[16]

The point being made here is that we have relied too much on the American myth—with its glorification of struggling ascent—and our traditional limiting contexts. The centrist believes that we need nothing fundamentally new as we move forward in history. But without new ways of coming to terms with the common good in our future, we shall simply continue to magnify both the goods and evils in our present approach. The present process may not suffice; it may lead to a paralysis in dealing with the future.

In conclusion, our nation, while dominated by a highly optimistic myth, has always had contrapuntal themes churning within it. While at first they were only a minor note, in recent days, at least in the literary tradition, they have become the major theme. The decade of the sixties particularly has revealed hard-to-ignore historical events. The wreckage of the past, the failure or refusal of ascent, and the closure of our future have called into question our innocent freedom from the past, our assumed self-initiative, and our belief in our infinite social and geographical landscape. Conventional responses include the leftist response, that of dissent, with its hatred of the myth and goal of supplanting the whole system; the rightist response, that of assent, with its refusal to see the dark side of the myth and its insistence that indeed nothing is really wrong; and the centrist response, that of balance, with its awareness of mythic ambiguity, but wrong assumption that the common good will emerge out of competing interests.

If the preceding has been an attempt at a description and analysis of the American myth and practice, then the following will be an interpretation of the *meaning* of the crisis.

NOTES

[1] R. W. B. Lewis, *The American Adam* (Chicago: The University of Chicago Press, 1955), p. 116.

[2] Daniel Boorstin, *The Americans: The National Experience* (New York: Vintage Books, 1967), pp. 169–219.

[3] Nelvin Vos, "The American Dream Turned to Nightmare: Recent American Drama," *Christian Scholars Review*, vol. I, no. 3 (Spring 1971), p. 196.

[4] Ibid., p. 199.

[5] Ibid., pp. 200–201.

[6] Ibid., pp. 201–202.

[7] Ibid., p. 59.

[8] Melvin Webber, "The Post-City Age," *Daedalus*, vol. 97, no. 4 (Fall 1968), p. 1097.

[9] Ibid., p. 1099.

[10] Ibid.

[11] Vos, "American Dream, p. 205.

[12] Edward Banfield, *The Unheavenly City* (Boston: Little, Brown and Co., 1970), pp. 45–66.

[13] Theodore Roszak, *Where the Wasteland Ends* (New York: Doubleday Anchor Books, 1973), p. xx.

[14] As cited in Gibson Winter, *Being Free* (New York: Macmillan, 1970), p. 146.

[15] Ibid.

[16] John C. Raines, "Theodicy and Politics," *Worldview*, vol. 16, no. 4, (April, 1973), p. 46.

Chapter III

The Nineteen-Sixties: Turning the Screws and Unveiling the Truth

The decade of the sixties seems in many ways to have marked a new stage in the long development of American religious history. The decade seemed to beg remembrance for having performed a great tutelary role in the education of America, for having committed a kind of maturing violence upon the innocence of a whole people, for having called an arrogant and complacent nation to time, as it were, and for reminding it that even Mother Nature is capable of dealing harshly with her children when they desecrate and pollute her bounty. There are good reasons for believing that the decade of the sixties, even at the profoundest ethical and religious levels, will take a distinctive place in American history. In summary, one may safely say that America's moral and religious tradition was tested and found wanting in the sixties.

> Sydney Ahlstrom
> *A Religious History of the American People*

THE HARD TRUTH

To feel that the events of the past decade have been tumultuous is one thing, and an important one, since it calls us at least to take seriously what we have experienced at the most elementary level. But it is quite another thing to understand the significance of what we have experienced. Our conviction is that the past ten years have been a moment for the unveiling of truth to the American people. The moment of truth is a personal, intensely interior event of discernment. It cannot be forced or imposed from without. But it most often comes to us precisely because of what external circumstances have forced upon us. We refer to these rough external circumstances as the turning of the screws, and we believe that it is necessary to talk about the interior revelation of truth in the same breath with the harshness of the tightening screws. Only as we recognize the intimate relation between the two—external crudeness of fact and internal sensitivity of understanding—can we hope to grasp what these days hold for Americans and for Christians.

If we are to recognize the moment of truth amid the turning of the screws, we must take a special stance toward evil, suffering, and pain, since these latter realities form the context in which much of the truth is disclosed to human beings. We do not overlook the testimony of goodness, love, and tenderness, since they too point to the very depths of human being and reveal to us what our life here on earth is all about. But even these moments of light and goodness take their place against the background of the evil and suffering that beset us at every moment. The gracious dimensions emerge from the wrestling with evil and they testify in the midst of the struggle to our essential meaning as beleaguered men and women—even when we seem to be on the losing side of the battle.

The special stance we are talking about requires in the first place that we acknowledge evil when we see it. This may seem elementary, but, of course, it is far from that, because our responses to evil often show that we refuse to acknowledge it for what it is. We prefer, for example, to interpret the blows of evil as if they were problems to be solved, or unexpected setbacks, oddities that can be disregarded. We prefer to dress evils in neutral, nonmoral language. We have been taught to do this, and not without reason, because a problem is much easier to attack and deal with if it is conceived to be a neutral entity. Alcoholism as a sickness that can afflict anyone is much more easily dealt with than alcoholism as a moral defect. As a disease, alcoholism receives the whole healing effort of society; as a moral defect, alcoholism subjects the poor victim to the taboos and rejection of his peers. But from another point of view, we know that our neutral conceptualizing is an escape strategy in many instances, thus often rendering our problems apparently more manageable than they actually are. We objectivize them, put them at arm's length from us, so that our encounter with defect and difficulty is never really able to penetrate the deeper dimensions of our existence and touch our personalities in any profound way. When neutral conceptualizing disarms yesterday's lies with the phrase "Previous statements on this subject are now inoperative," then all the advantages of the de-moralization of our problems have been transformed into demonic escape. In some cases, taking the problem out of the realm of morality helps us to survive better, because it focuses our efforts on problem-solving. To say that an event is evil means that the problem is like the tip of the iceberg; it is in actuality only the small one-tenth of the reality that lies nine-tenths hidden from view. To name a problem an evil is to issue an invitation—even an imperative—to search below the surface and probe the recesses of the problem-event. This invitation threatens us, whether the problem is on a personal scale or a monumental societal scale.

Acknowledging evil within the problems of our lives is just the first step, however. If we are to know a genuine moment of truth, we must reflect upon the evil event's significance to us, its causes, dynamics, and above all what the event tells us about ourselves and our lives. This deeper probing is also threatening to us, so much so that we often employ another escape strategy that we call "ideology." Ideology all too easily names events as evil and then goes on to "explain" them by scapegoating others for the evil, by projecting imaginary fears, engaging in the paranoia that sniffs a conspiracy under every stone, and stereotyping people and events associated with the evil. Ideology too facilely turns all problems into evils, and it thereby disarms the evil as surely as our neutral conceptualizing does. Ideology also holds evil at arm's length, rendering it lifeless and incapable of penetrating deeply into our self-understanding except within the tightly drawn boundaries of our stereotypes.

The reflection that we speak of, if it is to penetrate the problems that face us, must press more searchingly into the events that mark our recent common life. Nothing less is required than recognizing what Paul Ricoeur speaks of when he says that "Evil is supremely the crucial experience of the sacred."[1] In other words, events of evil are neither simply problems to be solved and put out of the way nor dread dangers that can be stereotyped, and thus boxed off in an equally safe manner. As an experience of the sacred, the encounter with evil unveils the mysteries of our limits—and our limits are the key to much of what our human being is all about.

Limits, in the first place, speak to us of the course we can run, the channels within which our lives must remain if they are not to perish. These limits are not self-evident, but must continually be tested and charted. There is something about a human being that will not accept a limit until that limit has been challenged and twisted and proven finally either intransigent or malleable and even unnecessary. Too quick an acquiescence to limits keeps human life less than it can be and thus ironically keeps hidden from us what the true limits of human being are. Rooted in this same indomitable resistance to limits that threaten to narrow and flatten life, however, is the equally irrepressible tendency to fantasize— not the fantasizing which denotes the creative, life-giving dreaming of man, but rather its perversion—the perennial misreading and distortion of the signals that our world sends us. This fantasizing sees limits where there are none and refuses to perceive the contours of the real limits that do exist. This fantasizing is grounded in the human being's self-consciousness, in his capacity to respond not only to the signals he receives from the world, but also to his own perceptions of and responses to those signals. To paraphrase Wallace Stevens, we live in our descriptions of the world and not in the world itself.[2] Responding to our own descriptions of the world is a source of human greatness and also the threshold of possible disaster. It is potentially disastrous because it means that we can fail to recognize the limits that sustain our lives. Humans differ from laboratory rats in a maze. The rat finally senses that hitting his head against the blank walls means that he has met a limit and must alter his course if he is to survive. Man may fantasize so ingeniously that his skull is cracked and bleeding before he comes to the same conclusion—if he comes to it at all! And it may be even more disastrous if man by chance succeeds in breaking down the wall of the maze, because he may very well conclude from this "victory" that he has conquered his limits when in fact he has simply deviated even further from his authentic existence and begun to fall headlong into the abyss. History is full of examples (and so are psychiatrists' offices and mental hospitals) of men and women who have been crippled by the blows of their world, but who nevertheless do not even sense the pain and who are by no means sensitive enough even to their own bodies to alter their ideas and their behavior. They have met the "problem" that was in fact "evil," and their insensitivity or damaged ability to respond has rendered the encounter shallow and destructive.

Limits are more than the walls of the maze through which our human lives traverse their years, however. Limits are also the experience of evil that brings us up hard against our own end. "End" has two meanings, both of which are applicable to our point here. End can mean the finish line, the termination, like the end of a movie, and it can also refer to the goal or meaning of the process. In the latter sense, we say, "The end of human life is to love," or we ask, "To what end are you subjecting yourself to such strict discipline?" These two meanings of the "end" correspond to *death* and *future*, since death raises for us the specter of termination, the *finis* at the conclusion of our own personal motion picture, whereas future poses the questions, "What is my life for?" and "Where is my life going?"

Now the rat in the maze asks neither about death nor about future. He simply perceives the unyielding wall and moves, as a consequence of what he perceives, in another direction. Humans are different, at least when they are actually living as *human* beings. We, too, must move and alter our direction, even if that move is simply to get a running start to jump over or beat down the wall. But we also ask the question, "What signals am I receiving about my *end*?" The depressed person will mean by this only the question of death, while the fantasist too often is asking only about his imaginary future. Authentic human reflection asks about both death and future. Does this problem or obstacle mean that I have in fact reached the limit of my life in this particular direction, under these specific conditions? Is this problem a sign that my physical, intellectual, emotional, spiritual death confronts me just now? If I am this sort of creature, subject to these limitations, subject to this kind of death, what is my future? Is it a future that backs off from this dead-end, to pursue another path? Or is it a future that will alter the conditions I am now in (say, by arming myself with ten companions and a battering ram) and demolish this obstacle? The sum of all these questions and their answers is reflection upon the meaning of human life, the particular limits or death that are unavoidably ours and the future within that death. Sometimes this reflection is an instinctive awareness which is seldom articulated, and it is manifested in the seemingly spontaneous sureness of judgment that characterizes a person of public action, while at other times it is the matter of deep contemplation which fills the diaries, the poetries, the literatures, and the philosophies of great men and women whose lives are seldom in the public realm.

Later in this chapter we will describe how the "forgotten realities" described in Chapter II are the problems that must be perceived as events of evil, the dead-ends in the maze that Americans are traversing. But now we push further into our description of the reflective sensibilities that are necessary if Americans are properly to understand the evils and pains of our common life and enter into the encounter with the sacred reality which those painful events open up for us. The sensibilities we refer to grow out of our awareness that our experience of the past decade unveils to us the truth about our end, about our death and our future as an American people. The problems and difficulties that we face are our world's way of turning the screws on us, sending up signals which provide the occasions for us to understand who we are by probing our possibilities in the face of obstacles, failures, and threats to our survival. These problem-events are the dead-ends that correspond metaphorically to the rats' maze. These problems are challenges to be solved, if we are to survive, but they are also evils to be understood, evils that invite us to encounter the depth and mystery of our existence. Sensitive understanding of that depth and mystery is also necessary to human survival.

It is beyond our understanding why being caught in the painful turning of the screws seems to be a prerequisite for human being to enter sensitively into the unveiling of the truth. The long history of mankind testifies that it is so, however, and reminds us that, whether we understand it or not, we must acknowledge that pain and truth are companions, that the person who is caught on the grinding potter's wheel is the more likely to see the truth—although even that pain is no guarantee that he will not repress what his mind and body tell him and instead fantasize himself into oblivion. The potter's wheel is a prerequisite, not a warranty, for the truth.

THE ENCOUNTER WITH EVIL IN CURRENT EVENTS

Grappling with the questions of the end—death and future—in our current experience leads us to questions about ourselves and our place in the scheme of things. Situations of difficulty prompt us first of all to consider just what we are—as individuals and as a society—and where we are presently situated in the overall setting of time and space. We call this the *question of location*. The question of location is cropping up with increased regularity nowadays as we bump up against limits which raise the question, "What's a human being for, anyway?" or "What's a human society for?" The occasion for these questions is always a specific one which confronts us with our end, such as, for example, the growth of cities, particularly in areas of great beauty which cannot, due to water shortage or atmosphere, sustain massive populations comfortably under any circumstances, let alone maintain their beauty at the same time. Is the population to be allowed to mushroom, demolishing the beauty and access to nature in areas like Southern California and Oregon, Colorado and Vermont? This is the question of death. The question cannot be answered without at least an unconscious response to the question of future. What is a San Diego or an Oregon *for*? What future should be planned for societies like these that feel the unavoidable death-in-limitations. In other words, what are the people, the human societies, in these areas *for*? What is their reason for being?

These questions are not timeless abstract qusetions. They could not even have been asked by human populations in previous periods of history in San Diego or Denver or Oregon or Vermont—at least not in their present form with their present urgency and significance. The citizens of these areas are not only located in space, but also in time, at a particular point in history, and a proper assessment of that time is crucial. Is this the last moment open for us to "save" those areas? Or is the time already past? Is a Los Angeles already past the point of retrieval, or a Chicago? Is it the case that New York and Lake Erie have already died, and the news has simply not yet gotten to us? Or is time more open than we think? Are the "Tourist Go Home" bumper stickers the nervous twitches of eco-maniacs who have misjudged the time-frame and who thereby really do threaten the necessary development of a society that depends on the technological expansion which these "maniacs" are successfully delaying?

If we insist that problem-situations are only the emergences of stubborn problems to be solved, obstacles to be cleared away—instances of what we and Aldo Leopold have called the "Abrahamic concept" of mind which moves only onward and upward, cutting down obstacles as they appear—then questions of location will not only never be answered, they will not even occur to us. The question of location ignored or passed by is also a moment of truth lost —a moment of truth about ourselves as creatures, who we are and where we fit into the overall scheme of being and history. The moment of truth opens up its possibilities for us when we see those problems as evils that confront us with our *end* and thereby invite us to probe beneath the so-called problems.

Even the few examples we have cited reveal to us that the question of the end is one of possibility and not defeat. The death, for instance, which Southern California even now envisions in its encounter with growth and development does by no means justify necrophiliac doomsday sermons. Rather, that encounter with death brings home with jolting clarity that perishing *is* possible, and under what conditions the region and its people may very well be devastated. But the vision of death also opens up horizons of alternative *futures*, and alternative futures go along with new paths of opportunity and fulfillment. Under the impact of the moment in which truth unveils itself, these alternative futures are indirect testimonies—which we perceive only in the most sensitive reflection —about who we are as human beings, where we are located in space and history, and what we are for, what we are intended to be, what our destiny is. These are questions that we are not clear about; they are being continually unfolded to us, if we have the eyes to see and the ears to hear. As a consequence, it is of survival-significance for us to reflect on our "problems," to see what they can unveil to us as occasions of "evil," about ourselves and the reality in which we live.

Probing the encounter with our own end is not exhausted by

questions of location. *Questions of dependence* also emerge. These questions come to the fore in our sensitive reflection, because as we ponder our death and our future we become aware of what is required for us if we are to actualize that future. In other words, we gain a sense for what we are most fundamentally dependent upon in our lives. The awareness of what we are dependent upon dawns on us in the very pain of being cut off from the sources that support us. Again, the dialectic between the turning of the screws and the sensitive reflective grasp of the truth shows itself when we face the loss of our support system; we understand most clearly, and sometimes even for the first time, how dependent we are on that system. Problems as such cannot impress this insight upon us; only evil can, because problems do not threaten us. Problems are neutralized, packaged dilemmas that can be processed for resolution, whereas evils open up for us ever-deeper recesses of mystery, the matrix in which we live out our many careers as individuals and our one career as a human species.

We take our deep dependencies for granted until they begin to be weakened, when evil cuts us off from them. We often recognize this common experience when a beloved person dies, or when an injury deprives us of a talent or activity that has been precious to us, or when a vital resource like petroleum is taken away. In any case we may be quite unaware of the dependency until it is lost. In our common experience as groups, the experience of dependency may be more elusive. If we recall an earlier example, we may observe the dependencies that are revealed when a beautiful region is subjected to overpopulation and development. At first, it may be pure pleasure at the setting and climate and economic advantage, based on geophysical coincidence, which makes the region attractive and serves as the basis for its growth. In this stage it may seem that life in the region is dependent upon "development"—growing population, tourism, industry, transportation, highways. But when the region has become saturated, the beauty despoiled by people, housing and recreation developments, and industry, when housing has become so scarce that prices allow only the affluent to move in, and environmental backlash takes away the pleasure of life—then what appears to be the ultimate dependency for the society? The very thing that has been lost by "development"—the beauty, the desirability for living? At one level, yes, but at another level, something still more profound emerges as that upon which the society is dependent, and that is a relationship of respect and harmony between the human population and the environment. This harmony is more basic than either the beauty and economic promise of the first stage or the need for development of the later stage of that region—the relationship of harmony was always a prime dependency, but it presses itself upon the awareness of the human residents only in the moment when it is threatened. The balanced and reciprocal relationship between the human population and the natural environment stands as a testimony about what it means to be human beings, an insight of self-knowledge that deepens the understanding of location.

For the religious person, and this includes the Jew and the Christian, the question of dependency is also the question of God. Centuries of Jewish and Christian experience have affirmed that in the negotiation with what he is dependent upon man has to do with God. The way of speaking has varied and the precise nature of God's presence in the dependency has not been fully understood, but the affirmation is solid. The father of modern Protestant theology, Friedrich Schleiermacher, writing around 1800 in Germany, equated "utter dependence" with the religious dimension of human life, laying down the axiom that when man is aware of his utter dependence and its sources, he is "experiencing" God.[3] Martin Luther, two hundred and fifty years earlier put a similar idea in classic form in his Large Catechism. He wrote: "To have a God is to have that to which we look for all good and in which we find refuge in every time of need."

We draw closer at this point in our reflections to the heart of Ricoeur's insight that evil is supremely the crucial experience of the sacred. It is evil that threatens to cut us off from the ultimate supports of our existence and thus it is evil that lights up for us the points where God has chosen to enter our lives. The most intimate and yet most fearful aspect of the experience of evil is its invitation to reflect upon and gaze into God himself. These are not activities over which we exercise autonomy, but rather are the way in which we are grasped ourselves by the dependencies of our lives. That being-grasped is both sublime and terrible, and this may explain why we so often prefer to speak of "problems" rather than "evil," since we can exercise autonomy over the "problem-solving process." And it explains why, if we do acknowledge evil, we then go on so frequently to stereotype it, so that it cannot get hold of us and bring us to gaze upon the very ground of our existence which threatens to slip away. In this being-grasped by the ground of our dependency which is God, we see the relationship between the turning of the screws and the unveiling of the truth drawn so tight that the two are almost one. As with the Hebrew prophets and with Job, in the moment of near-destruction, when the ultmate support of life is almost totally gone, we are suddenly aware that we are just as totally in the presence of our God.

For us, the encounter with the ultimate source of our dependency reveals that death lies in the direction of defying God, since that proves to be a defiance of our own nature, whereas our future is opened up for us when we follow the beckoning of our deepest dependency, because the power of that future is in fact God. The ground of our deepest dependency tells us what we are for, for what we are here, namely, to follow the lead of that ground or source.

Within the context of quite specific events of difficulty, we experience evil which carries within it the possibility for an encounter with our own end, under the forms of death and future. We have painted the context of this encounter in broad strokes, suggesting how, under the impact of the harsh—even devastating—blows of these events of evil, we may, if our spirit is graced with strength and reflective insight, glimpse the truth as it unveils to us the reality of our location within the larger scheme of things, who we are, what we exist for, and our place in history, and also the reality of God's presence for us in the ground of our deepest dependency. Against this broad background, a third and final set of questions are illumined when we grapple with our end. These are *questions of the meaning of our entire past*, and they are intimately related to our location and dependence, because those other insights that have grown out of our reflection upon death and future give us the key for interpreting the meaning of our past history.

We ask the questions: "Where have we been in our past experience—as individuals and as a society?" "What does that history mean?" "How shall we grasp hold of its myriad of happenings?" "How does it all fit together?" The answers come back: Our history is the story of our following the lead of the power upon which we are ultimately dependent or from which we are deviating, of conforming to that which we have been made to be or resisting our very own purpose. We lay hold of the bewildering array of uninterpreted and even contradictory events in our past from this point of view: by relating them to what we have learned about why we exist at all, to the ground of our deepest, ultimate, dependency. What we have learned through reflection upon our location and our dependency forms our arsenal of values.

From our grappling with the harsh turning of the screws, we gain a set of criteria by which we judge and interpret our past and project our future. These criteria give answers to three questions which are of paramount importance for interpreting our past history: Where have we been? Where have our strengths really been evident? and Where have we gone wrong? These three questions are of concern to every American today, and we are suggesting that the Christian (or the Jew) will find the answers in fuller reflection upon the nature of the evil that confronts us in our current experience, what the encounter with that evil tells us we are about, and what it unveils to us about the power of God in our midst, upon whom we are dependent for life.

RETRIEVING AMERICAN HISTORY

What we have called the questions of location and dependence make great intellectual and moral demands upon us. They make us pause to reflect seriously on the shaking events we have experienced in the past ten years. We must pick up the questions of the meaning of our past—the questions of *where we have been, our strengths,* and *our going wrong*—and discover the wisdom they hold for us. On the first level, we seek, as straightforwardly as possible, to answer these questions.

We refer, for example, to our ecological example of population growth and regional development in the western United States. Our ultimate dependency has been revealed as a covenant relationship of belonging between the physical and natural environment and the human population. In response to the question, "Where have we been?" we have pushed forward largely oblivious to our responsibility for the environment, coming perilously close to the point of no return in our irresponsibility, and now facing the unpleasant task of disciplining ourselves and planning our future development in a way that will restore the balance and reciprocity between every element in the ecosystem. Our evident strengths show up in the wisdom of some conservationists, city planners, and legislators who have provided a basis upon which current efforts can build. Where we have gone wrong we discern in every decision and act that violated our contract with nature.

"Going right" and "going wrong" in our past history are measured against the basic reason for what being really is, against our destiny. We study our past, therefore, for clues that will throw further light on the possibility that is within us and the destiny God has prepared for us. This destiny is what we are dependent on. Our past history is not simply a record of rights and wrongs, of merits and demerits awarded for wise or irresponsible actions, nor is it primarily a source of proof-texts or justifications for what we are doing today. Americans are particularly prone to use history as proof-text—the liberals for their actions, the rightists for theirs. Above all, our past history is the document which serves as basis for retracing our career to discover what we are called to and what power of God sustains us in that call.

Nevertheless, in retracing past events—both those where we went right and those where we went wrong—we look not so much at what did in fact happen as at what could have happened. Not in the mood of daydreaming over "what might have been," since such fantasy is a pathology of its own, but rather in order to discern what possibilities—intrinsic to our being and sustained by the power of God—lie unheeded and even unknown or repudiated in our past development. In other words, what knowledge about the possibilities of our own being is embodied in the historical record? In order to carry out this quest we need a new kind of study of history. It is not enough to accumulate "the facts," although such efforts are indispensable to our quest and should not be scorned; without the basic spadework, no one can understand history. Nor is it adequate simply to chart the "rights" and "wrongs" of our past, although this, too, renders a real service to our understanding. The recent spate of so-called revisionist histories of post-World War II America fall largely in this category. It is good and necessary for us to debunk our previous heroes when we have venerated them too blindly and uncritically. The "other side" of the cold war story, as the Kolkos[4] and the Halberstams[5] tell it, and the insight that Camelot was only one side of the Kennedy era—these revisionist tellings of the American story stimulate and cleanse our reflective vision, even though we remember that the debunkers themselves are subject to their own critiques. The revisionists sharpen our sense of what going right and going wrong in history means, just as the mainline histories which they criticize did prior to the debunking.

Gathering the facts and organizing them, however, and judging the rights and wrongs must lead to the deeper and more reflective judgment about what our very nature as persons and as a people demands of us and what that nature enables from us. Mere storytellers provide us with clear imperatives (sometimes) for present action: Don't repeat the mistakes, be vigilant against the culprits, and carry on the grand tradition. It is a more or less sophisticated version of the "good guys versus bad guys" theory of history. The problem of this way of telling the American story is that it results in unhelpful stereotypes which stand in the way of real understanding. A by-product of this stereotyping is that certain events and persons in our past are rendered positive and negative. We are encouraged to feel proud and ashamed of our past—and things are left there: *Do* emulate the events and persons of pride, *abhor* the shame.

What we need to understand is that going right or wrong and being proud or ashamed—*at their deepest*—grow out of whether we have been obedient to the possibilities that are ours, and that obedience occurs only in basic harmony with the ground upon which we are dependent for our being. What fact-gatherers, court historians, and revisionists alike must help us to do is to discern from the past what is revealed about those possibilities and about that ground of our dependency. When we do achieve this discernment in the study of our past, we have adequately retraced our history; we call this an *authentic retrieval* of our history. It retrieves history from shallowness and unhelpfulness, it retrieves it for our use.

We utilize many mechanisms of retreat from clear historical reflection, many modes of self-deception to keep ourselves from gazing into the truth. Perhaps it is because, like individuals, we as a society sense that even though the truth about our possibilities is the key to our liberation, to be fulfilled as human beings, that truth is hard to handle; it shakes us, as Moses was shaken before the burning bush or on Mount Sinai—and we would rather not face the shaking ground of truth. The references to Moses are not misplaced, since the truth of our possibilities is also the truth about the power upon which we are dependent, that is, God-present-in-our-midst. And so we suppress the past from our conscious memory.

Concealment and suppression, then, are the two greatest obstacles to our adequately retracing and retrieving the American past. Concealment blocks out "alternative pasts," and with them the way in which alternative insights into our possibilities can work for alternative futures. We want to know how it could have been different in the past, not in order to wish absurdly that things had gone differently, but rather as an insight into how things may go differently in our future.

There is no chance whatsoever that the unveiling of the truth of our past will emerge in a shaking and healing way for us except through the give-and-take of open and vigorous dialogue among all of us who remember. The Indians at Wounded Knee must be as free to contribute to the dialogue as the General Custers—and each must be fully free to correct the remembrances of the other. Suppression of dialogue about our past is to violate the rules of our American game; such suppression is anti-American, antihuman, the most pernicious form of self-mutilation and masochism, since it renders the truth about our possibilities absolutely inaccessible.

To eliminate suppression means that information must be freely disseminated, by whatever means, just as it means that voice must be available to all, overclass, underclass, rich, poor. Finally, it means the end to authoritarianism in the dialogue. Authoritarianism is the antithesis of dialogue. Authoritarianism implies that one or more of the parties in the dialogue is beyond reproach and stands above questioning; it assumes that some parties in the dialogue can be squelched and put down.

The retrieval of our American past is in one sense neutral and "value-free." That is to say, this retrieval aims at unveiling the truth about our possibilities and the power of our dependency out of which those possibilities arise. This means that it is not first of all concerned to convict certain parties of sin and to praise other parties for their virtue. Inevitably, certain events will be items for regret, certain persons and incidents will appear as shameful repudiations of our own best selves and the ground of our dependency which is God, whereas others will seem to be heroic and virtuous. There is no reason to avoid these judgments. But at the same time, there is every reason to emphasize that the real lesson of history is what it reveals about ourselves, so that we can reshape our future. That real lesson is lost when first of all we set about the task of inflicting guilt or heaping praise for our past. The guilt and praise are intrinsic to our remembrances, but they must be transcended and transformed into a deeper sense of what our past tells us about ourselves and our possibilities and responsibilities for the future.

In another sense, the retrieval of our past may appear to be an example of "positive thinking," since it concentrates on our possibilities, rather than on our failures. What follows in this book should dispel the feeling that we are here setting forth a naively "positive" approach toward America and American history. It is true, however, that our past, with its positive moments and its failures, is a testimony to the power of what we are called to be, our possibilities. The failures turn out to be even more horrendous because they are betrayals of these possibilities and treason against the calling of our destiny. But we view the failures nevertheless for what they tell us about that calling, rather than as realities in and of themselves. What they tell us is exceedingly painful, however, and alters the face of those possibilities, creating new imperatives.[6]

PRESSURES FOR RETRIEVAL IN THE SIXTIES AND THE SEVENTIES

The past is irreversible, in the sense that it has happened—it cannot be put on the "instant replay" and done over again—and also in the sense that we have to accept its consequences and live with them. But the irreversible character of the past does not mean that the past has exhausted our possibilities, nor that the "might-have-beens" of the past cannot be resurrected and made effective today for the future. We may have today augmented the possibilities for decisive action that we missed in an earlier time—say, in redressing the problem of hunger—with our technology. Or, conersely, we may have minimized our maneuvering room, as, for example, in providing adequate housing for dispossessed groups, now that our urban centers are more crowded and deteriorated than they were fifty years ago. But the possibilities are still there, to be spelled out under new conditions, with new discernment and resolve. Those possibilities retrieved from the past are incorporated with the possibilities that we perceive distinctive to our own times and our own vision, as we attempt to project ourselves in our own future.

The sixties and the seventies have been a particularly intense period of the turning of the screws for the American people, and, as a consequence, they represent one of those "special moments" in our common history which we may probe, with discipline and pain, for the unveiling of the truth about the power of God upon which we are dependent as a nation and the possibilities that are ours in our dependency. They may even be one of God's *kairos* events, a time prepared for revelation.[7] The concrete happenings of the sixties and the seventies, and the shocks they have brought to us have been set forth and analyzed in Chapter II. Now we must probe the material from that chapter and seek to crystallize a few central insights that emerge from the past decade of American history—insights that do not give us "facts" about ourselves as a people but that illuminate who we are, fundamentally, and what is at stake in the crisis which now engulfs us.

THE LOSS OF INNOCENCE AND FINITUDE

It may be, as Robert Bellah contends, that every social critic in our country since 1900 has declared that America has just now lost its innocence. Nevertheless, the turbulence of the sixties hammered into the consciousness of broad sections of the American mainstream as never before the awareness that the "can do" position is, after all, finite.[8] This is perhaps the most obvious implication of the events and issues we discussed earlier. The Adamic myth which has expressed so much of our understanding of ourselves has been innocent of finitude, and the American ethos has effectively muted the indigenous witnesses to that finitude. In Joseph Sittler's terms, we were a people without an eschatology. We believed in the future, but it was a future that would never end—a kind of eternal and open-ended present. The shock which the sixties brought to us was that the future does curve back upon us, that we do have limits, and that those limits mean that we cannot escape the consequences of our own actions, including actions taken long ago, by previous generations.

It was one thing for us to celebrate the brawling, tainted, and yet "chosen" Adam (the "Abrahamic" people, to think of Leopold's term[9]). This was the American of Carl Sandburg's "Chicago Poems," who liked to pick a fight and won our hearts in his doing so. After all, the brawling, irresponsible Adam was also hog-butcher of the world. Like the sacral king of the Orient, he caught up the destiny of the world in his life and actions, and so if he fed, cared for, and lighted the way for the peoples of the world, his brawling expansionism at home and abroad must also somehow be the fulfillment of their own best destiny. This Adam was tainted, yet his goodness was inexhaustible, and so his defects, if they were more than robust fun, were but clouds on the horizon, no larger than a man's hand, and therefore not significant for the American myth. Even those who, like Lewis's Party of the Fall, did sense the significance of Adam's defects could not illuminate for us the finitude of an America placed in a crowded, technologized world. Nevertheless, those voices are witnesses whom we must retrieve and listen to over again for a clue as to the meaning of America—in the time they wrote and today. The dark underside of Adam is visible to more of us than before, but that is not the major threat we feel. We sense now that the field for our development is not endless, we cannot simply rely on our ability to outrun the foes within and without. Rather, Adam's defects now assume the proportions of an "anti-Adam" that coexist within the finite body that is our society.

It is certainly not that previous generations of America were unaware of Adam's darker side, as we pointed out in Chapter II.

The significant thing about the sixties and the seventies is that the loss of innocence about ourselves and the awareness of our finitude became irreversible for large masses of Americans.

Earlier decades knew about the ecological problems that attend technological development just as they knew about the deprivaiton and injustice that the American society was inflicting upon blacks and other minority groups. But that knowledge was not effective in altering the consciousness of the people. With respect to the ecosystem, we know that irresponsible use of resources was rampant on a continent-destroying scale in the nineteenth century, and we are aware that the technology which was arising then was already exhibiting its antihuman tendencies. The farsighted conservationists and the industrial reformers and social workers often saw deeply and accurately into the emerging state of affairs. We can now understand (and retrieve) their vision in a new way. The conservationists were not just setting aside land for parks and preserving beautiful landscapes for later generations, nor were they simply employing agricultural techniques for improving crops and delaying erosion. They were attending to the fact that we are a people that is dependent upon a "belonging" relationship to the earth and its subsystems. Earlier generations of conservationists were in no position to see the vast proportions both of that belongingness and of its violations.

Similar developments apply to the relations between the races in our society. Earlier generations, particularly among the abolitionists prior to the Civil War, perceived with unerring accuracy the threat of our racist policies. We have concealed much of their testimony. Our myths, for example, depict the Fourth of July oratory of past generations as unrelieved affirmation of the course of American life, if not utter jingoism. We have suppressed the memory of the heroic abolitionist reminders on the national holiday that we were abandoning our ideals in our treatment of blacks. We recall William Lloyd Garrison's Fourth of July address in Boston in 1829:

> Every Fourth of July, our Declaration of Independence is produced, with a sublime indignation, to set forth the tyranny of the mother country, and to challenge the admiration of the world. But what a pitiful detail of grievances does this document present, in comparison with the wrongs which our slaves endure! In the one

case, it is hardly the plucking of a hair from the head; in the other, it is the crushing of a live body on the wheel—the stings of the wasp contrasted with the tortures of the Inquisition. Before God, I must say, that such a glaring contradiction as exists between our creed and practice the annals of six thousand years cannot parallel. In view of it, I am ashamed of my country. I am sick of our unmeaning declamation in praise of liberty and equality; of our hypocritical cant about the unalienable rights of man.[10]

In the same way, we have suppressed the fact that speeches were given on the floor of the United States Senate during the Civil War charging that Protestant clergy were responsible for the hostilities because of their abolitionist activities![11] We can retrieve and transform the memory of these events in our past for guidance in our own day. But it is only in the past decade that the soil of the American mind has become fertile for the awareness to which those early voices bear testimony. In our day the innocence which suppressed the truth about our society's treatment of blacks and other minorities has almost universally been wiped out. Here, too, the belonging relationship of the races has been lifted to awareness.

In these two dimensions of our common life, the relations between man and the environment and the relations between the races, we can illustrate how an earlier innocence has given way to realism. It is for our generation to feel the full impact of what this finitude demands—namely, that our society lives in a discrete, circumscribed world (this is finiteness vis-à-vis our environment), in which the life of every individual and group is reciprocally related to every other (this is finiteness vis-à-vis our human family). In both cases, it is belongingness that comes to the fore as the primal relationship that governs our existence. The covenant of belonging to our world and other people is a fundamental element of the dependency that enables us to live.

The stereotypes of infiniteness have hidden this deep truth from us as a people, despite the voices of prophecy from earlier times. In the sixties, continuing in the early seventies, these stereotypes broke down with a crash of illumination that revealed to us more about ourselves than most of us really wanted to know. We can examine in some detail two of these stereotypes of infiniteness—infinite whiteness and infinite masculinity.

Black and White

The underlying stereotype of Americanism has been that all Americans are one or another shade of white. The American dream has not really embraced any other color. The liberal idea of integration reckoned with colored minorities as dark-skinned whites and spoke of integration into the dominant white society as the goal. The sixties brought to our mass consciousness what many had already known—that the American melting pot had not really melted as we thought it would, and most of all, it would not melt everything into infinite whiteness. It became disturbingly clear to nearly all Americans that the nonwhites possess cultures of their own, even within these United States, that they even speak their own linguistically distinct forms of English within our midst. In short, these nonwhite peoples possess a cultural integrity of their own, even if their culture is intertwined with, even dependent upon the white cultures.

Black Power is the name we have given to the most powerful assertion of black cultural integrity. Black Power asserted the integrity and thus the finite validity of the social existence of blacks in America, and at the same time it demonstrated the finite validity of the dominant white culture. In the process, it retrieved from the past on the one hand the validity of the white abolitionist protest and on the other the protest of the unyielding black resistance (expressed in the history of figures like Nat Turner, Denmark Vesey, Harriet Tubman and in the spirituals and the blues).[12] Despite the separatistic strand within the Black Power vision, that vision is primarily a message about coexistence, about the reciprocity between finite cultural groups within our society. Black Power is about integration and in this it affirms the liberal dream in a limited way.

The emergence of Black Power transcends and transforms, however, both these historical traditions—abolitionist and black protest on the one hand and the liberal dream of integration on the other —in the very process of validating them, and this transcending is a critique and redirection at the same time. Integration on the new terms is not between "white-skinned whites" and "dark-skinned whites." It is between white-skinned whites and black-skinned blacks. Integration on the new terms is not subsumption under and absorption into the dominant white and middle-class society, but rather the creation of a new multiracial (and perhaps genuinely interracial) society. Finally, integration on these post-1960 terms is not a process of liberal whites helping crippled blacks to enter the white society. It is rather blacks—both weak and strong—grasping their future and making it their own. As Jesse Jackson once said in our hearing, Black Power is saying "good-bye" to our white brothers and sisters for a time, so that at a later time we can come back, stronger blacks and stronger whites, and say "hello" to each other on new terms.

Black Power envisages the constructive rebuilding of a multiracial society in concrete economic, political, and cultural terms in a way that was simply not possible for either the fiery preachers and conductors on the underground railway or the defiant slaves and the inspiring creators of the spirituals and the blues. The protest is validated, but transformed into a concretely operational social planning. To paraphrase Bayard Rustin, Black Power transcends protest so that its energies can operate a factory, meet a paycheck, and educate the rising black population.

Here we have a clear view of what retrieving our past is about. These traditions—protest and integration—are retrieved under the conditions of the present moment and *pro-jected*, carried forward, in a form that is appropriate to the present. This projection recovers in the present these past traditions and experiences from their concealment, from what our public consciousness has tried to forget. The brutality against which black and white alike protested in the nineteenth century can no longer be repressed and maintained as a silent minority witness. It will out, and we pay the wages of that past sin today, with higher interest rates. The abolition of injustice will be painful, because the wrath of three hundred fifty years of repression will have to be lived through, and that means that the new integration will appear on the surface to be more a catastrophe than a healing. Retrieval and projection of our American past will not permit us the illusion of thinking that we can avoid this catastrophe; if it did, it would mark itself automatically as an inauthentic retrieval and projection of our past. By the same token, if we can bear it and resist further suppression, retrieval and projection point us toward an authentic future that justifies our dreams and our language of hope.

We may pick up a thread of our earlier discussion and say that, when the stereotype of infinite whiteness is destroyed, then the covenant of belongingness is lifted up more clearly than before. Under the old regime, there was a belonging—blacks "belonged" to the whites as chattel. The new vision affirms that the relationship between the races is so intimate that "belonging" is the proper designation, not as chattel, but as two creatures in the same ecosystem belong to each other. Or, as James Baldwin images the relationship in his novel, *Another Country*, as man and woman belong to each other—that is, they are destined for each other and they have a stake in each other, as well as a claim to lay upon each other. The retrieval and new projection of our past experience opens up new horizons and profundities of belonging between the races in America. The vision is so deep and so close to the very essence of our American existence that it is as frightening as it is thrilling. An instance of finitude shatters a false stereotype of infinitude, only to reveal a truer vision of the finite and Infinite.

Men and Women

The stereotype of infinite masculinity is also instructive for understanding our American existence. This stereotype has also functioned in a way that concealed the finite realities of our common existence. In a strange way, shattering this stereotype has brought us to arguing both for unisex and for the indestructible integrity of women as women. The unisex argument is an understandable and necessary assertion that differentiation between the sexes which serves to put women down or deny them equality of opportunity for human development is illegitimate and "against nature"—"nature" in this case meaning the inherent right to self-fulfillment. The insistence that women possess an indestructible integrity grounds itself in the truth that the wholeness of femininity is intransigent to efforts to demean or masculinize it.

As with the encounter between the races, the meeting of the sexes on the terms set by the women's liberation movement shatters a false infinitude for the sake of finite realities that can be set free to interact with each other. This new interaction emancipates the finite realities of man and woman to live together creatively within the reduced—and yet expanded—arena of society. As with the black movement, there occurs in the current encounter between the sexes an urgent and profound dialectic between separation and unity. The unisex symbolic points to the unity of man and woman within the human enterprise, the separation testifies to the inviolability of the integrity of each.

The fact-gathering stage of historical recollection of the relations between the sexes has not proceeded as far as it has in the study of the races in America. But already it is possible to say that a retrieve and projection of the past similar to what we noted above with respect to blacks is in order. Again, this will be a retrieve and projection that validates both protest and reconciliation. The retrieve will not only validate the eradication of what is called male chauvinism, thus affirming a major thrust of the women's lib concern, but it will also explore the concrete, finite ways in which men and women can interact. These finite interactions will be discrete, in some ways trivial, but painful and also significant for rebuilding the covenant between men and women. The pain will come as the stereotype is cracked and cast aside. The separateness of the sexes will be revealed within a larger unity that speaks, however, of a new kind of belongingness of the sexes to one another. "Belonging" will be transformed, as past traditions of men owning women will be cast totally aside and the reduction of women to a status of sex object that belongs to the conquering male will be repudiated (and the reduction of men to sex-and-success objects will also be rejected). A deeper, even more inexplicable belonging of the sexes to one another will be opened up, and this will constitute an opening up of a new kind of infinite mystery and possibility between the sexes.

Although the older images of the woman's role as invisible helpmeet and subordinate object must be repudiated, the destiny of women is not simply to become "like men," in pure competition. The destiny of women can hardly be that of masculinizing their femininity, but must include the femininizing of the male order as an integral part of a rising equality of opportunity for women. Thus, the sameness of the sexes as imaged by unisex is affirmed and denied. In assuming their equality (and in this sense sameness under canons of justice) with men, women must change the masculine order, they must contribute a new dimension to what it means to be human (and in this sense deny their sameness). The older role understood belongingness as important, even if it almost fully misunderstood the dynamics of that belonging relationship between man and woman, whereas the new liberated image—clearly perceiving the inadequacy of the older role—must learn what belonging means and forge a new covenant between the sexes.

Finiteness and Public Visibility

We could extend what we have explored in some detail with respect to the new finitude of perspective on relationships between the races and the sexes in America. Similar stereotypes have existed in other areas, as, for example, in nearly all professional/client relationships. We see evidence in the medical professions, where doctors encounter patients who suddenly challenge professional pretensions to a kind of infinitude of authority and wisdom, as well as in the practice of law, social work, teaching, and the church. In the sixties, the professional class discovered a complexity of finite relationships interacting in new ways.

International events also contribute to our loss of innocence concerning our national existence. One of the chief lessons of the Indochina War may lie in the bluntness with which it confronted Americans with their limitations within the world community. We may yet understand that the phrase "peace with honor" in Vietnam was a code word disguising the negotiated settlement of the first war America has clearly lost—and ironically against a foe much weaker than we. The bloodiness and shame of this war should not blind us, however, to the new moves in the old "balance of power" game of international politics, since these moves, which brought détente with China and Russia, were again a recognition that American infiniteness within an unlimited political environment is no longer viable as a dream. Again, the détente as well as the war and current international economic developments quicken our awareness that we are living in a world in which we are finite, and that we are caught up in interactions with other finite entities. The

Third World is just now entering our awareness, but it will contribute, perhaps even joltingly, to the awareness of finitude that we have described. John Q. American will—in one way or another—become aware that the shirt on his back has been made possible by the bare backs of those who live south of the equator, whose share of energy, resources, and wealth we have been consuming. This new awareness will challenge the infinitude of our appetites and of our exploitation in a way that parallels what we have learned about ourselves in others areas of our life.

The same dynamics may be present in each of these areas of new awareness: The emergence of a new finite antagonist within the world of heretofore dominant groups at one and the same time shatters the previous pretensions to infinitude which the dominant group entertained concerning itself and also reveals the immense, mysterious, and complex world of finite interactions to which the dominant group and its antagonist are "doomed" to live. This initial experience of shock rearranges the whole landscape of social existence, often engendering new animosities, even hatreds. At the very least it brings a host of bewilderments. But being doomed to complex finitude of relationships in the place of phony infinitude serves the emancipation of all the groups in our society—if the possibilities of finitude are lived out bravely.

None of this would be possible except for the fact that heretofore *publicly* invisible and unimportant groups in our society entered the public realm, stepped onto the stage of public history. The groups were always present, but we suppressed their reality through the concealment of our own history. Blacks, Chicanos, women, homosexuals, Indochina, the Third World, are now on the stage of world history in a way they have never been before, and this is what makes the difference. Once on the stage, they become integral to the political process, legitimated partners in the action of our social existence.

LOSS OF INNOCENCE AND IDENTITY CRISIS

Our discussion up to this point would be misleading if it left in the reader's mind the impression that the events of the sixties are relatively manageable instances of encounters between groups that challenge each other within the larger context of our society. We

mean to describe the loss of innocence and the shattering of the
stereotypes of infinitude in terms that lay bare the poignancy and
trauma of the confrontation with finitude.

The confrontation is traumatic because it threatens the very
images of identity which the parties to the encounter entertain
about themselves. Each group in the confrontation is faced with the
prospect of nonbeing. Ripping away the stereotype by which the
dominant group perceived its own omni-competence, by which it
pretended to bestow meaning on everything and everyone, is tanta-
mount to saying: "Things are not what you think they are; you are
not what you think you are; you are not the only one who bestows
meaning; we have our own way of giving meaning to the world!"
The threatening character of this confrontation is obvious—and it
is even more so when it hits the dominant, pace-setting groups in a
society, in our case the white middle class and males.

To be confronted with this testimony by an antagonist is to be
asked to change in a fundamental way both our behavior and our
image of ourselves. If it is true that we live in our *descriptions* of
the world rather than in the world itself, then current attacks upon
our infinitude are really attempts to change the world we live in by
altering its description. This in itself is a monumental and painful
task, and it is what the events of the sixties and seventies are
demanding, not only of the heretofore publicly "invisible" groups,
but also of the dominant white culture. There is still more, however. The call to change both behavior and self-image is prompted
by the awareness—through confrontation—that what we have been
has carried within it, along with its good, elements so evil and
destructive that their very presence calls into question who we
thought we were as Americans. The threat posed to us as America
is that if we do not alter our behavior and self-image we face
nonbeing, because even though we thought we were pursuing a
"good, American way of life," what we have been has included a
dimension that violates and will certainly destroy our own understanding of what it means to be America. So, it is not only the
trauma of being faced with the threat of having our identity
images ripped away and the prospect of change which shakes our
national existence. It is also the horror of recognizing that in the
past we have not been who we thought we were and who we

wanted to be—a recognition that has been brought home to us by the shaking events that we went through in the sixties and which extend into the seventies as well.

The loss of innocence about ourselves and our past and the crashing in on us of our own finitude thus become at the same time a huge identity crisis for the American people. We have been confronted with evil—not just problems—in our recent history, and this confrontation has unveiled the truth about who we have been and who we can be. Questions of location, dependency, and the meaning of our history are now ones with which we can deal—in pain, yes, but also in freedom—if we do not permit ourselves further concealment and suppression.

As Americans we witness for the first time in our history a confrontation with our death. Other civilizations have confronted this phenomenon, some of them many times. We have lived at a level of relative spiritual superficiality. We are in fact facing the deepest spiritual challenge of our history, the task of defining ourselves as a people in the face of our real limits. This spiritual challenge is both fearsome and inviting, it holds both danger and promise. But we must remember that the narrowing of our sphere through the awareness of our finitude makes possible a genuine advance in the defining of our future that renders our possibilities much richer and fuller than that of the young, untamed, naive Adam.

THE IMPASSE OF THE AMERICAN SYMBOLS

Although the description of our present American situation points clearly to the challenge of a new self-definition of America in the face of the loss of the identity that has governed our lives up to now and even though that challenge holds promise for Americans, the situation today poses a problem for which Americans are peculiarly ill-equipped. The problems that face America today and inflict pain upon our common life all point to the presence of error, failure, and self-deception in our past, and these are precisely the phenomena which the symbols of our American identity, our public philosophy, cannot deal with very well.

For example, in the case of racial and ethnic minorities, we are faced with the dilemma that there has been a consistent practice of depriving millions of Americans over many decades of basic freedoms and opportunities. But our public philosophy holds, on the contrary, that these freedoms and opportunities are the inalienable rights of *all* men. The philosophy says nothing about why it is that certain human beings are denied inalienable rights. The word *inalienable* is at the root of the dilemma, because it makes any denial of freedoms and opportunities automatically contradictory.

Or, economic problems: The public symbols of our identity speak of opportunity for all, of the success of the free enterprise system to provide for all its citizens. We include the symbols of the New Deal which assure us that after the Great Depression we finally redistributed the wealth so that poverty need not exist. Now, two generations after the New Deal, with fifteen per cent of our people still under the poverty line of income, the wealth is not so evenly distributed as we would like to think. The graduated income tax is still not equitable. Or we cite, for example, the very epitome of the free-enterprise system, George Romney, who brought Rambler Motors into the Big Four of car manufacturers. In his 1971 report on the housing and urban development program, in which he had been involved for four years, he said that his programs for housing the poor were failing miserably. We have no symbols for explaining these sustained economic inequities and failures.

Let us take the war in Indochina: We Americans have no way of comprehending for ourselves why we should be defeated or why we might wage a mistaken war. We simply have no public language for even discussing these possibilities.

Or the "have-nots" who refuse to conform fully to our WASP ideals: Our philosophy has said: "There is a great American race for improvement and economic well-being. If there are have-nots, it is because they are hindered from running the race; we must be sure that everyone has a chance to get to the starting line and run the race." The assumption is that everyone really wants to run the America race. We have no symbols for explaining to ourselves that some people might want to run the race in their own peculiar way or refuse to run at all on the track that most of us have run on.

In other words, the American philosophy stated in our Declaration of Independence and the Constitution, together with the Bill of Rights, and contained in our public symbols of identity, does not have the images to account for precisely the kind of identity crisis that we are called upon to deal with today. It is as if the times were conspiring to hit us at our most vulnerable point. This is not a farfetched image, if one accepts the opinion that disease (physical or psychological) generally hits the organism at its most vulnerable point. What this means is that America is not only facing the pain that comes from suffering through problems that are so intense that they hit like blows in the solar plexus, but we are at the same time suffering from an identity crisis which those blows have precipitated, because the public symbols that tell us who we are cannot account for these blows and help us to understand them.

This inadequacy of the symbols of our identity is not unique to Americans, but it has not plagued every nation. We may contrast this inadequacy with some other nations. The Marxist identity symbols, for example, do provide one way of dealing with past errors (although not very adequately, in our opinion) in terms of the dialectical movement of history. This symbol speaks of the movement of history from feudalism through the bourgeois period to the proletarian stage. Errors and failures in the present system can be laid at the feet of bourgeois elements which are anti-revolutionary, anti-socialist, or revisionist. This symbolism must be combined with a vigorous tactic of scapegoating. Although it does not always work and becomes increasingly less plausible as the years go by, it is a set of internal symbols for explaining failure and evil at home. A few groups in America also adhere to these Marxist symbols, and although their number is small, they are growing, perhaps even among groups that are not really radical.

We might also point to the ancient Hebrews, whose symbols of identity included the idea of disobedience to the covenant which accounted for the causes of national failure and mistakes and for the subsequent punishment at God's hands and the experience of his wrath. It may be that the ruling groups in Israel did not generally accept these symbols and that the prophets who enunciated them were champions of the "have-nots" in Hebrew society. The fact remains, nevertheless, that the symbols were there and frequently used as the Hebrew self-consciousness tried to come to terms with its public life. Many Americans also subscribe to these

Hebrew symbols, and, as we shall discuss in the next chapter, some observers even suggest that we take this covenant into our public philosophy. Nevertheless, we can hardly say that the Hebrew symbols belong to the public philosophy that works in the society as a whole at the present time.

Finally, the ancient Greeks possessed a set of symbols which included the tragic vision, with its idea that the cruel gods would sooner or later thwart any man who followed his natural desires and ambitions. Thus, any man, including the leaders of society, could expect eventual misfortune and tragic failure.

Later, these symbols were exchanged for another set, which asserted that life on this earth is continually plagued by evil and misfortune because of the inherent wickedness of bodily life.

Since we do not have public symbols of this sort, our identity crisis entails working through the problems of embarrassing and unexplainable evil in our midst in terms of new symbols from our own American philsophy or borrowing from other symbol systems, as the radicals are trying to do with the Marxist symbols. How this will come about we cannot predict, but it must come about if we are to survive as America. No society can live with unexplained evil when that evil threatens its very identity. What is clear is that recognizing this dilemma and working through to new symbols will in itself be a painful and agonizing process. We are only at the beginning of this painful process, and we can expect the suffering to get worse before it improves. Since, more than any other, the white middle class has been the bearer of American identity, this identity crisis will hit it harder than any other group.

The state of affairs that we have just described may be called a *symbolic impasse*. A significant chasm between our experience and the images we have customarily employed to "explain" our experience presents us with the task of acting on the basis of our new image of ourselves as a finite people without symbols to guide that action. We need a context of symbols which point to our new identity and relate that identity to our previous history.

FREEDOM AND CONTROL, A CENTRAL DILEMMA

There is yet another decisive disclosure about common life that the sixties have brought to the surface—the possibility that our magnificent freedom has outrun itself.

Technology has increased the wallop by which the evil spin-offs of the dream have hit us. The imperatives of growth and profit have driven already great centers of private power, with their fantastic technological potential, to unguided and uncontrolled expansion. In the process more and more competitors drop out of the race because they can't keep pace with the increased need for capital and new technology. Increased production stimulates increased consumption and vice versa. Living in harmony with the natural world becomes increasingly difficult, even if new rules of the game are thought up.

As Reinhold Niebuhr has argued, civilization (technology, science) magnifies the possibilities of human creativity and tragedy, but in no way guarantees either. Put another way, history cumulates the problems of man and does not solve them. Technology has magnified beyond measure the thrust of every ascending corporate entity, pressing it to slashing competition for available resources, know-how, and markets. There is no logical end to the thrust. The open social and geographical spaces are gone. Mobility increases —people continue moving and consuming, without having a real dwelling place of their own. The contradictions in the American dream, which were hidden by the illusions of innocence and limitless social and geographical space, have come home to roost. The age-old problems concerning the harmonious relation of the one and the many, and the guidance of both into the future, have hit America. These problems have been exacerbated immeasurably by the magnifying powers of technology.

We have destroyed or damaged many of the traditional contexts of belonging in our headlong race to ascend. We have not cared for the land, the "place," from which we came. Family contexts have been eroded in our increasing mobility. Communities, neighborhoods, towns, farms—all are in danger of being churned up as the myth drives us forward. Civilizing traditions are cast off.

In short, the dynamism of our life is overcoming the sustaining matrix of communal existence. The perennial continuities that give form and substance to our shared life are ripped apart by the pressure to keep moving. A solid sense of "place," of one's own *axis mundi*, is increasingly rare. Our sense of dependence on the "givens" of life wanes. Freedom is destroying belonging.

The challenge of the third hundred years of the American

nation is to develop a responsible control that embraces and insures both freedom and belonging. Control without freedom would destroy the American tradition as well as lead to stagnation. It must reflect the assent and consent of the people. Control without belonging is irresponsible and heteronomous. However, since we have a myth and a rationale that reinforce the notion of freedom and none that legitimates an intentional control of the future for the sake of preserving structures of belonging, our task and dilemma are acute.

The central dilemma concerns freedom and control. The present structure of the American myth and its limiting contexts—which in the short run maximizes freedom—cannot deal with the need to shape and guide the future in such a way as to insure the survival of structures of belonging—and thus freedom itself—in the long run. In order to control and shape the thrust of American technological society in the future, such a massive concentration of power in government hands would be necessary that it would jeopardize radically both freedom and authentic belonging. The control needed to provide long-run survival of belonging and freedom would cancel liberties in the short run. Considering our knowlege of other societies' experiments with short-run limitation of human freedom for the sake of a future justice, equality, and freedom, we cannot be overly pessimistic.

This dilemma produces excruciating tension. Some smaller societies with homogeneous populations have combined freedom and control in somewhat promising—although not too promising —ways. The Scandinavian countries and perhaps England have made interesting attempts in that direction. But their citizenry seem rather unhappily bored and unimaginative. Control may be taking its toll. Besides, their approach will not be appropriate for a society of our size and diversity.

The Soviet Union and China have made their decision for heteronomous control and belonging. India is not yet industrial. Other modern European countries and Japan will face the same problem that America faces now.

How can American society deal in its own way with the tension of the dilemma posed above? We would propose that there are three inadequate ways of dealing with it. The first two—the proposals of the left and the right—relax the tension of the dilemma by doing away with one pole. The third—the centrist stance—has full awareness of the dilemma, does not dissolve the tension, but tends toward the mistaken belief that we can muddle through under some providential umbrella.

The prescriptions of the right are being played out by the current administration. The wraps are being taken off the larger private corporate impulses while government is withdrawing from concerns of the public sphere. We are going to rely more and more on the private sphere. Even some of the traditional limiting contexts are being weakened. The strong are given freer rein with the assumption that as they grow stronger they will carry the weak with them. Concern for limiting and guiding economic growth is nonexistent. We press with more uncontrolled momentum into a future that cannot under those conditions be gracious. The one horn of the dilemma, the need for a more intentional future, is lopped off. The far right wants even the traditional limiting contexts weakened. The moderate right is willing to move into the future with the tradition unmodified. Even the President is ready to suspend the rules to protect his unimaginative vision of the future.

The defenders of the right continue primarily to come from the established controllers of wealth. It is understandable why they think that the free expression of their own interest will benefit all. The marginal and threatened lower middle classes are more volatile and less decipherable. They are at one and the same time the source of reform and reaction. But as Lipset has argued in *Political Man*, when threatened, workers and small businessmen and farmers become fertile fields for the right. They feel the pressure of the lower classes below them and perceive them as a threat. They can move either way. Thus, the workers who showed a preference for Robert Kennedy before his assassination voted for Wallace after it.

At any rate, the right tends to view our society as though it were still in the nineteenth century—in the height of the bourgeois revolution. It relies even now on what Tillich calls "technical reason" to carry the day. Private initiative harnessed to technical reason is sufficient. This illusion blinds the right to what we have termed the dark side of the American myth. It bridles at any thought of control or guidance by public means. It provides a sure way toward continued erosion of the belonging pole of American life.

The left makes different mistakes. It is ready to concentrate enough political power in public hands to control private power and guide the industrial machine into the future. It has little sensitivity to the proper limits of politics or to the dangers of concentrated political power. It proposes that public power usually be in the hands of some innocent, oppressed group—the working class, the blacks, the Third World in our midst, etc. The leftist proposal for the American scene is not particularly threatening now and probably never will be. Unfortunately, however, it siphons off the energies of many valuable people who ought to know better, who ought to be aware of the bad scene of ideologically straight-jacketed collectivist societies that are neither just nor productive. Moreover, the left gives the right the perfect occasions for the use of "scare" tactics.

The left, which dissolves the tension of the dilemma by lopping off the freedom pole, is rooted in a radical minority of the intellectual classes and in the nonapathetic elements of the lower classes. As in the case of the right, they believe that if they had control things would be better for all. Contrary to the right, however, they would not wed their innocence to technical reason but rather to *planning reason*. Being on the short end of a fragmenting bourgeois society, they see the possibility of planning a new order of justice and prosperity. But the performance of centralized governments using planning reason has been dismal. And, of course, elemental freedoms and liberties are given up, never to be returned, for the sake of some future goal. Any future American attempt at control and guidance cannot take the classic leftist route. The new American attempt must arise out of authentic structures of belonging and freedom.

Finally, there is the centrist position that is particularly seductive to the prosperous middle classes and to the rising lower middle classes. Those whose achievements in American life have outstripped their expectations make up a great share of this persisting center. The majority of the intellectual community are at home here too. The mark of the centrist fallacy is its partial or full awareness of the dilemma we described above. It knows our technological society is unguided and out of kilter. But it treasures the private freedoms and opportunities it has under the superstructure of the great concentrations of private power.

The centrist perspective has no real answers. It falls back on the old American idea of gracious future that will somehow get us off the horns of the dilemma. Perhaps out of the dynamic process itself, perhaps out of an unexpected breakthrough to a less turbulent post-industrial society, or perhaps through some unseen harmony that is operating below the surface contradictions, we will make it through.

The dilemma of freedom and control illustrates the crucial need for new dimensions in both the American myth and its limiting and sustaining contexts. In our technological society, the old limits cannot contain the thrust of private, corporate groups whose dynamic is increasingly subverting the structures of belonging that sustain us. New kinds of control must be found. The control—or guidance—that we are talking about cannot be based on the assertion of narrow self-interest. Thus far, American interest group theory has assumed that the common good will emerge out of the mutual limitation of self-interested groups in competition. But that assumption no longer holds. For this competitive interplay does not protect—indeed it destroys—the realities of community that lie at the root of man's collective existence. Structures of belonging are not represented, and certainly not nourished, by this interaction of self-interest. Something new is needed.

Summing Up

In this chapter, we have asserted that the experience of the last ten years has been an encounter with evil in our public life which is God's moment of truth for the American people. This moment of history unveils for us just where we partakers of the American dream have traversed in history and what fruit we harvested from our journey through three hundred years of peoplehood and two hundred years of nationhood. God's moment of truth for us uncovers, we believe, three fundamental issues confronting us: (1) our finitude as a people, concerning which we may never again entertain our traditional naiveté; (2) the inadequacy of our public symbols to deal with the brute facts of evil, failure, and self-deception that have precipitated our present identity crisis; (3) the dilemma we face in bringing our cherished power of freedom and advance into balance with the finite world which is our support-system and which bestows our very being upon us. Finitude, identity crisis and symbolic inadequacy, and the dilemma of freedom and control— these are bedrock realities that God apparently will not let us shunt aside in our national life. If we are to define ourselves as a people, we must meet these basic elements head-on.

NOTES

[1] Paul Ricoeur, *The Symbolism of Evil* (Boston: Beacon Press, 1969), p. 6.

[2] Cited in Robert Bellah, "American Civil Religion in the 1970's," in *A Creative Recovery of American Tradition*, ed. W. Taylor Stevenson *Anglican Theological Review*, Supplementary Series, no. 1 (July 1973), p. 9.

[3] Friedrich Schleiermacher, *The Christian Faith* (Edinburgh: T. & T. Clark, 1928), par. 4.

[4] Joyce and Gabriel Kolko, *The Limits of Power: The World and U.S. Foreign Policy, 1945–1954* (New York: Harper & Row, 1972).

[5] David Halberstam, *The Best and the Brightest* (New York: Random House, 1972).

[6] Readers familiar with German philosophy will recognize that a great deal of this section utilizes the thinking of Martin Heidegger and Jürgen Habermas. We refer the interested reader to Martin Heidegger, *Being and Time* (New York: Harper & Row, 1962); and Jürgen Habermas, *Knowledge and Human Interests* (London: Heinemann, 1972).

[7] We refer here, of course, to Paul Tillich's celebrated notion of God's proper time in history. See his *The Protestant Era* (Chicago: University of Chicago Press, 1948), chap. 3.

[8] Robert Bellah, "American Civil Religion," p. 12.

[9] Aldo Leopold, *A Sand County Almanac* (New York: Ballantine Books, 1970), p. xviii.

[10] Quoted by J. Earl Thompson, Jr., *The Religion of the Republic*, ed. Elwyn Smith (Philadelphia: Fortress Press, 1971), p. 272.

[11] See George Huntston Williams, "The Ministry and the Draft in Historical Perspective," *Una Sancta*, vol. 25, no. 1 (1968), pp. 3–40.

[12] See James Cone, *The Spirituals and the Blues* (New York: Seabury Press, 1972).

Chapter IV

The Christian Agenda
for Religious America

Two roads cross the Hoop of the World. One begins in the East where the days of man begin, crosses the Hoop and ends in the West, where the days of man end. This is the hard black road of worldly difficulties that all men must travel.

If there were only one road and that a black one, this world would not be much, but there is another road, the good red road of spiritual understanding. It begins in the South where the power to grow lives, because one must grow to become spiritual. This good red road of spiritual understanding goes straight North across the Hoop of the World to the region of white hairs and the cold of death. *Where this good red road of spiritual understanding crosses the hard black road of worldly difficulties, that place is holy.* There springs the tree of life and it shall fill with leaves and bloom and singing birds, and shield us.

> A statement, common to the traditional Sioux prayer garden, found at the John G. Neihardt Shrine, Bancroft, Nebraska (italics added).

THE RELIGIOUS DIMENSION OF AMERICAN LIFE

The burden of our essay has been the defining of America, and in the process of our reflections we have dealt with two dimensions of the defining enterprise. The first is the more or less clearly discernible tradition of how Americans have in fact defined themselves as a people in the centuries since the immigrants first touched North American shores. We are painfully aware of how selective and simplistic we have been in summarizing that tradition of American identity. Nevertheless, it stands as the way we presently read our history. Americans have overwhelmingly (but not unanimously) defined themselves by reference to the so-called dream—the people who shook free from a limiting past in a struggling ascent toward

93

the realization of promise in a gracious, open future. Even the considerable minority that dissented from the crass, one-dimensional manner in which this dream was preached had to define themselves in terms of it, just as the Amerindians and the blacks who possessed different dreams have been forced to redefine their indigenous visions over against the dream that the European immigrants fashioned. This dream-definition of America emerged from the experience of persons who were continually called upon to be frontier people, whether that frontier was a wilderness to be tamed and settled, an economic system that needed to be fashioned and operated, a social order to be established, or frontiers of mind and spirit.

For these earlier generations, putting together the dream was a process of defining America in the midst of their rugged existence, whereas, for us, it seems that their definition is a finished product, our heritage. It is also a millstone around our necks, which we did not fashion, but which, to the contrary, fashioned us. This is deceptive, however, because in reality defining America is always more than heritage, since it is also a rugged contemporary task. Every generation has had its millstone from the past to contend with, as well as its vital, helpful heritage. As it has been said of the ancient Hebrews, every generation of America stands on the shoulders of the Fathers, but it has to define itself afresh, so that it becomes America anew for itself.

The events of the present age will not permit us the luxury of simply scrutinizing the dream, gathering together the strands of our identity from the past generations of America, and then accepting or rejecting it. Nor do they allow us the option of a rootless transnationalism. Rather, recent history prods us vigorously to get on with our own business of defining America.

Self-defining, the process of seeking and forming identity, is, moreover, through and through a religious enterprise. We affirm what a whole generation of Christian theologians has emphasized, that the entirety of human life is lived in the power of God. The work of the Spirit of God manifests itself in the activity of the human spirit, and the goal of that Spirit is to bring the Creation, humankind included, to its fulfillment, to the destiny that it shall become when its possibilities are made actual. For an adequate understanding of our perspective, it is important for the reader to grasp the significance of this affirmation, that all of life is lived in God's power, moving us toward actualizing the possibilities we have been given and fulfilling them. This means that all of the essential activities of human beings share in the power of God himself. Among these activities are those that have to do with identity. The human spirit, as it struggles through to its identity, enters upon the ultimacies of human existence, and in these ultimacies, the Spirit of God undergirds the human spirit. In an older manner of speaking, we would say that in these ultimacies, man experiences God. Most recently, Harvey Cox has spoken of religion as "that cluster of memories and myths, hopes and images, rites and customs that pulls together the life of a person or a group into a meaningful whole."[1] Cox is pointing to the same realities of human life and its lived religion that we are. We are referring specifically to the American nation and its quest for the myths and images that pull the nation's life together into a meaningful whole and which place the individual's life meaningfully within the ordered whole which is the nation.

Paul Tillich has given decisive theological attention to the significance of the quest for identity.[2] He has shown how identity has to do with the integration of the person or the group which enables them to assert their distinctive being in the world that surrounds them, permits them to embody in actuality the being that is within them. The search for identity is nothing less than this, the struggle to get clear about what we really mean for ourselves, into what meaningful whole our lives really fit, and to get that meaning into our decisions, our actions, our life-style, in a concrete and effective manner. The framing of the American dream has been exactly this. As the American people have defined themselves over the generations, they have given symbolic expression to what they mean for themselves, and they have sought (sometimes with terrible and destructive consequences) to embody that meaning concretely in their national and international life. Since this quest for identity and definition is one of the most important occasions for grappling with the Spirit of God, and one in which God's Spirit is active along with and in the human spirit, we cannot avoid the conclusion that the process of defining America is itself a religious experience.

We must go further and say that the religious dimensions of the American search for definition—like all such quests—are immeasurably deepened by the encounter with evil that gives decisive character to our generation, just as it did to the Civil War generation. No effort at self-definition is seriously carried out without facing up to the threat of being cut off from the mainsprings of identity by evil in one form or another. When we confront this evil squarely, then we understand what the power of God is all about and what it means for our identity. This is part of what Americans faced in the sixties and continue to face, and these years are forever a religious peak for the nation, if only we can understand the truth that they intend for us.

America, in other words, is living out its present days in an inescapably religious setting, faced with a religious task. America will respond religiously, that is clear. The question is, What shape will its religious response take? Even those who fancy themselves irreligious or nonreligious will be caught up in the religious response. The question is not whether there will be a religious response, but whether it will be good religion or bad, adequate religion or inadequate. All Americans have a stake in the current crisis, and the Jewish and Christian communities nowhere show forth more powerfully their solidarity with their secular brothers and sisters than in their particular concern with the religious task of defining America. Jews and Christians do not ask their fellow Americans to leave their daily tasks and "be religious." On the contrary, by remaining where they are and defining their national existence in their ordinary tasks, Jew, Christian, and secular American alike enter most significantly into the religious task that confronts us. There is nothing more urgent for Americans at this juncture in history than their identity—their redefining of themselves as a people.

Jews and Christians have definite ideas about what the proper religious response is. In expressing their own distinctive concerns *within* their commitment to the common task of all Americans, Jews and Christians will perform their greatest service to their God and to their nation. What this means is the concern of the present chapter.

Unfortunately, we cannot in this essay explore more fully our basic affirmation of the presence of God's power in our common life as Americans. Nor can we engage in extended argumentation over Ricoeur's thesis that the encounter with evil is an experience of the holy. We must make some important distinctions, however, if our position is rightly to be understood. We are not saying that there is a one-to-one identity between that upon which we are most dependent and God. The relationship between God and his created world is far too complex and our minds far too inadequate to allow us to assert simplistically that "God is . . . " (supply whatever seems to be the ultimate upon which we are dependent). But this qualification does not dilute our conviction that in the actuality of our most fundamental dependencies *we have to do with God*, and that in a real and forceful manner.

For those who wish to pursue the philosophical and theological complexities of the ways in which we may know and talk about the presence of God in our world, we mention Langdon Gilkey's *Naming the Whirlwind: The Renewal of God-Language*.[3] Gilkey reflects at great length on God's presence in our experience, and he concludes that any attempt to make our human existence totally secular, without any reference whatsoever to transcendence or ultimacy simply falsifies what even the would-be secular person actually experiences in everyday life. So writes Gilkey about the theological task: "We are concerned with our experiences of ultimacy as an aspect of our ordinary existence . . . hoping to uncover the sacral dimension in man's secular life."[4]

The powerful, unmistakable actuality of the experience of God's presence in our ordinary life, however, does not mean that it is a simple thing to point to this presence or talk about it. Gilkey goes on: "Since such an 'object' [that is, the sacred, God's presence] is and never can be directly 'manifest' in an essence in the stream of experience," an interpretive "process must be undertaken to uncover it. As we shall see, the essential character of the religious dimension is that it manifests itself in secular experience negatively and at best indirectly, *through* other things that appear directly."[5] Furthermore, since we are caught up in the midst of this ultimacy which is the foundation of our lives, that upon which we and our existence are dependent, we cannot grasp hold of it. It surrounds *us* and grasps *us*, we cannot hold it in the palm of our hands. As God spoke to Job, from the whirlwind:

"Gird up your loins like a man, I will question you, and you shall declare to me. Where were you when I laid the foundations of the earth? Tell me, if you have understanding. . . . On what were its bases sunk . . . ? Or who shut in the sea with doors, when it burst forth from the womb . . . ? Have you commanded the morning since your days began, and caused the dawn to know its place, that it might take hold of the skirts of the earth . . . ?" (38:3–13).

Job was perfectly familiar with the realities of earth and sea and dawn that were spoken about out of the whirlwind; in fact, he lived in the midst of those realities every day of his life; but he could not speak directly about their foundations and origins. We know the experience in which we are caught up, but we cannot grasp the depths and the breadth of that experience, because the depths and breadth are infinite and we are finite; they sustain us, we do not sustain them.

It is not only the vastness of our experience in its ultimacy that renders our talk about God difficult, but also the fact that, when we talk about our ultimate dependency, we are talking about something that is inseparable from *ourselves*. We all have experienced the irony of being able to know and talk about ourselves, the reality that is closest to us, only indirectly! The difficulties of gaining self-knowledge are symbolized by the physical fact that we cannot even look directly into our own faces. We can never even know how we really appear physically in our world—we must use mirrors and pictures to gain a view of our own appearance! We need other persons and events in the outside world to help us to know ourselves, to help us understand the dependencies that are at the core of our being and the power of God that touches us in them.

The theological character of our work is manifest in our willingness to assume the risk of being wrong and nevertheless take up the task of interpreting ordinary American life in these days in terms of its ultimacies and pointing to God's presence in that life. The elements of our interpretation lie (1) in our assessment that the primal myth of the civil religion is indeed a vehicle of divine disclosure to American experience; (2) in our understanding of what the sixties and the seventies have revealed about the American dream and its actualization in our society; (3) in our conten-

tion that the experience of America in the past decade is fundamentally an encounter with evil; and (4) in our conclusion that
the basic issues that seem to be emerging from the encounter with
evil have to do with the dawning awareness of our finitude, with
the deeply rooted symbolic problem that clouds our identity, and
with the root problem of whether our thrust toward freedom can
be linked with the planning and control that are necessary for our
long-term well-being. This task of interpretation is the burden of
the previous chapters. The effort *to point to the presence of God*
more clearly, as he manifests himself in the midst of our experience and our crises, is a task of reflecting upon the actualities of
American experience that we have already discussed and taking the
leap of describing the ultimacy which (to use Gilkey's words)
manifests itself negatively and at best indirectly through these
events that are so directly real to us.

THE MODES OF GOD'S PRESENCE IN AMERICAN EXPERIENCE

The symbols of American identity, gathered together as they are
in what we have called the American dream or the primal myth,
have emerged out of the people's response to the power of God in
their corporate history. Consequently, these symbols give us a clue
as to how God has in fact made himself available as a powerful
presence in the distinctive experience of the American nation. This
clue is only partial, and we must subject it to intense criticism at
every step, but we must first of all understand what the dream does
reveal about God's presence.

We get at the positive witness of the American primal myth by
noting what it is, at very bottom, that we are on the brink of being
cut off from in the encounter with evil that marks our current
times. In the encounter with evil, the bedrock dependencies distin-
guish themselves from the lesser ones. Sometimes these lesser
dependencies are very much cherished and we give them up only
with great regret, even though they owe their high place on our list
of priorities to our own illusions about who we are and what is
necessary for our existence. These lesser foundations of our existence are often very desirable, even necessary, but the encounter
with evil reveals that they are not ultimates, not the absolutely

essential and fundamental source of life upon which all else depends. We recall our earlier example of the crisis in growth and development that faces scenic areas in the western regions of our country. Without any question economic growth, development, and tourism are important for those regions. But the current crises reveal that life in these areas is not ultimately dependent upon this development, but rather that existence of persons, land, *and* development depends ultimately on something else—the covenant relationship between man and ecosystem.

We must ask, very broadly, What does the primal myth of America reveal about the ultimate dependency of the nation and its people? The answer to this question will point at least indirectly to God's power in our national life. In our reading of the tradition and also the current decade of experience, we see the presence of God for America in the power of the *future* to which America is called and in the power of *dedication* which that future demands.

We find negative testimony to the enormous trauma which alienation from future and dedication brings to Americans epitomized in the words of two American scientists in recent years. These statements sum up the sentiments of millions of Americans who are anguished in the face of the threatening break of our ties to what is ultimately necessary for our existence as a people. The first statement is from Nobel Laureate in Biology George Wald, who in his famous speech to students during the 1968 Harvard revolts put his finger on the underlying reason for the unrest: "I think that I know what is bothering students. I think that what we are up against is a generation that is by no means sure it has a future." Wald brought home in a powerful way the torment that surfaces when the absence of a future becomes an experiential reality for people. A scientist, past sixty years of age, he was saying that being cut off from the future is a terrible thing.

Margaret Mead provides the classic utterance of the woe of being cut off from the possibility of dedication. She writes in an essay on the future of mankind: "Most of the young people of the world are worrying about the meaninglessness of their *own* lives. They need purpose, and they are living on in society where the transmission of *commitment* has broken down." Here is the anthropologist, another sage over sixty, who has distinguished herself both as an academician who can share in and speak for the most current and common realities of experience and also as an older person whose understanding of the younger generation and whose hopes for it outstrip for the most part that generation's own imagination. (We remember her dictum that the older generation is under obligation to let itself be taught by the younger.) She speaks of the youth of the world, but what she says is epitomized in American youth. She speaks of meaninglessness, and she means thereby the sense of the loss of a future. The outcome of this loss of future is the loss of our ability to command dedication or to deliver it. An older generation without a future cannot transmit a sense of the beauty and necessity of dedication, whereas a younger generation without a future cannot mobilize its energies behind a dedication that, deep down, it knows is essential.

The Power and the Promise of the Future

The primal myth of American identity is nothing if it is not a celebration of the future as the ultimate reality of our national existence. This perception, as we have said, put us on a linear course in contrast to the prevailing cyclical national myths that dominated previous nations—and it did so long before Marxism performed the same feat for the societies of the East. The American symbols zero in on the centrality of the future from a variety of angles. The future offers the freedom and opportunity that belong inalienably to all men and women, just as the future promises the benefits of the economic and technological colossus to all our citizens. In lifting up these dimensions of the future, the American myth is the vehicle for the transcendent reality of the indeterminate uniqueness and freedom of man and also of his right to share in the fruitfulness of the earth. Freedom, uniqueness, opportunity, and distributive justice are at stake here, and the American declaration is that the future demands that we obey these virtues, even as the future promises their increase. The national identity includes within it the sense that these values are universal; the mandate of the future is that America should be a beacon to the nations, exercising its power and freedoms for the good of all men. This vision of the future is not simply that the future will be gracious, that is, that it will crown our efforts with success, but also that the future will continue to be open. This openness grounds the freedom and self-determination essential for the American identity.

Frances Fitzgerald, in her description of the contrasts between the American national myth and that of the Vietnamese, has spoken vividly of this American attitude toward the promise of the future: Americans "believe in the future as if it were a religion; they believe that there is nothing they cannot accomplish, that solutions wait somewhere for all problems, like brides."[6] She goes on, although many Americans question this national myth, "The optimism of the nation is so great that even the question still appears as a novelty and a challenge."[7]

The depth of our dependence upon the power of the future becomes agonizingly clear now, when we seem, as Wald says, under threat of losing it. The revelatory character of the events of the past decade, as we have outlined them, illumines how close we are to being cut off from the future that shines through the American primal myth. This revelation presents us with our participation in evils that are shameful by any standard: injustice based on racial discrimination, the devastation of an Indochina War whose justification is at best ambiguous and at worst criminal, the pain and poverty caused by maldistribution of goods and economic discrimination in a society of abundance and free enterprise, and the reckless laying waste of people and land in our rush toward profit and development. By any standard, we say, these realities become disclosures that bring us to remorse and shame. But there is also a more particular anguish that accompanies the confrontation with these facts in our society, namely, the sense that in each one of these evils we can feel the American vision of the future slipping right away from us. We see our hope for the future ground to dust before our eyes. For a people that has imaged itself as the new Adam, the chosen people sent on the errand of fulfilling the future for all mankind, it is difficult to imagine anything more traumatic and disillusioning. As we suggested, when we spoke of America's identity crisis, the trauma is real because loss of the future is loss of our identity.

We are, if we are to continue in our particular identity, totally dependent upon this power of the future that has been the motor of our national existence. That we are totally dependent upon it means that without the vision of the future we would cease to be America in the essential meaning of that word *America*.

This sense of the ultimacy of the future is manifested concretely in Abraham Lincoln's position on the slavery question, as William Wolf has documented it in Lincoln's debates with Stephen Douglas. The Founding Fathers laid down a charter of freedom and equality of opportunity for *all* men, said Lincoln. They compromised their charter and allowed slaveholding for pragmatic reasons, because otherwise not even the charter would have been adopted. The Northwest Ordinance of 1787 abolished slavery in new areas, and for Lincoln, the mandate for his time was to continue that thrust (this in spite of Lincoln's personal feelings that the blacks were not his political and social equals). On these grounds, he forcefully attacked Douglas's Nebraska bill, which would have permitted the territory to determine on its own whether to have slaves. Lincoln knew that the expediencies of the 1770s *had* given that very same right to the southern states, but he believed just as surely that the vision of the future which the Declaration of Independence and the Constitution embodied would not permit any further extension of the states' rights which the Southerners enjoyed on this question. The debates with Douglas were in 1858. By December, 1862, in his annual message to Congress he had broadened his understanding, so that he was thinking not only in terms of the future vision embodied within the American dream, but rather (to use William Wolf's words) of "the special destiny of America freed of slavery as a means to the advance of freedom and democracy over all the earth."[8] In the text of Lincoln's speech, it stands thus:

> A nation may be said to consist of its territory, its people, and its laws. The territory is the only part which is of certain durability. "One generation passeth away, and another generation cometh, but the earth abideth forever." It is of the first importance to duly consider and estimate, this ever-enduring part. ... Fellow citizens, *we* cannot escape history. ... The fiery trial through which we pass, will light us down, in honor or dishonor, to the latest generation. We *say* we are for the Union. The world will not forget that we say this. We know how to save the Union. The world knows we do know how to save it. We—even *we here*—hold the power, and

bear the responsibility. In *giving* freedom to the *slave*, we *assure* freedom to the *free*—honorable alike in what we give, and what we preserve. We shall nobly save, or meanly lose, the last, best hope of earth.[9]

And in the next month, he issued the Final Proclamation of Emancipation. The point we wish to make is that Lincoln's words over a five-year period on the slavery question indicate that he was following the thrust of the future (which for him was explicitly the thrust of God). That future led from the colonial period in which eloquent ideals were enunciated, but not put into practice, through to his own days, in which he rejected Douglas's attempt to cut back even further on the practice. In his own Emancipation Proclamation, he extended the ideals on into the continuing future in which he viewed the American freeing of the slaves as an example for the entire world. Lincoln's position in these circumstances, we insist, is an epitome of what the American primal myth essentially demands.

This power of the future is first among those realities upon which America is ultimately dependent, if she is to remain America. For this reason, the power of the future, with the freedom, opportunity, affirmation of individuality, and justice that are rooted in it—this power of the future is a mode in which God has manifested himself to the American experience. This manifestation has been celebrated in the primal myth of our nation, and its centrality for our identity is thrown into sharp relief by the events of the past decade which threaten to cut us off from the essential American future.

As the power of God in our national existence, the vision of the future also illumines our location in history and the meaning of our total history as a nation. It functioned this way for Lincoln in the example just recalled, clarifying for him that his age was part of the continuum between the colonial legacy and the demands of the mid-nineteenth century. It revealed to him *what might have been* in 1776 had not expediency ruled the course of events. Further, his awareness of the pull of the future taught him what his action should contribute to the totality—to fulfill the heritage and to hasten a universal movement of freedom, to make the "might have been" of 1776 an actuality in 1863. So, we can say, too, that

America's total meaning is wrapped up in the realization of a future that was unleashed in the initial visions which we have pursued and yet betrayed throughout our history. For example, in our economy, we have developed a technological apparatus which for the first time in history makes the full scope of our vision of abundance seem to be a real possibility. But at the same time, we must learn to interpret correctly our two hundred years of history to see how grossly we have betrayed our possibilities and how this betrayal is largely responsible for our economic problems today. We must retrieve our past, uncover the lost "might have beens," and be obedient to them today.

Or, in another area, whites do not learn black history simply to malign the whites who enslaved blacks and held them in suppression for centuries. Rather, we learn also to understand how we have for two hundred years most often engaged in the kind of direct and indirect racism which threatens to make a mockery of America's vision of the future. This history of ours, therefore, is not simply a history of injustice, but a mirror-image of our vision of the future and of our dedication to and/or betrayal of that future. In explicitly religious terms, this is the way we must speak of our faithfulness or unfaithfulness, as a people, to the God who is efficaciously present in our common life. And from this view of history we gain perspective on the imperative for the years ahead —renewed faithfulness to the future that burgeons within us.

Dedication and Sacrifice

The vision of the future to which the American myth has witnessed is a future in the hands of a God of order, law, right, and judgment. Many students of the American traditions have observed the sternness, the relentless demanding character of the deity. Not primarily a God of grace and forgiveness, he demands strenuous, even sacrificial efforts from those who are called to make his work their own. Even the sensitively reflective Abraham Lincoln knew God primarily as the inexorable God of Providence. To quote once again the memorable second inaugural address in 1865:

> Yet, if God wills that [this mighty scourge of war] continue until all the wealth piled by the bondsman's two hundred and fifty years

of unrequited toil shall be sunk, and until every drop of blood drawn with the lash shall be paid by another drawn with the sword, as was said three thousand years ago, so still it must be said, "The judgments of the Lord are true and righteous altogether."[10]

Not all Americans who have contributed to the primal myth have spoken so poignantly and transcendentally about God, but most of them have shared the sternness and righteousness of Lincoln's picture.

This kind of God demands dedication, commitment, even sacrifice. Although the vision of the future has often been debased, turned to chauvinistic ends, transformed into a justification for selfish greed and lustful brawn, a sense of discipline and the cost which the future exacts have also been rooted in the primal myth. The ascent toward the gracious future is a *struggling* one. One dimension of the struggle is epitomized in the energetic, highly self-disciplined pursuit of the future's promise—the style of a Horatio Alger, a young Lincoln, the campaigning Kennedys, the relentless Vince Lombardi. This is the athletic discipline, Aldo Leopold's "Abrahamic mentality" in that it struggles, takes what comes, and rises to the top more often than not.

There is another dimension of this sacrificial dedication which is symbolized by martyred heroes of America—Lincoln and Kennedy struck down by assassins as they carried out the responsibilities that the dream has placed upon them, Martin Luther King shot as he pursued the dream for us all. The sacrifice of the heroes is ennobling, according to the primal myth, and it calls the nation once again to its task. The central role of Memorial Day and the two great cemetery shrines of our land—Arlington and Gettysburg—is to remind us of this sacrificial motif.

The image of dedication and sacrifice as struggle, almost an athleticism, is not necessarily superficial, since it, too, embodies the fullness of human energies as people seek to be faithful to their possibilities. But it is a partial and generally insensitive mode of fulfillment. The motif of complete sacrifice, involving death and sometimes rebirth, is not universally prevalent in our national consciousness. Moreover, this motif of sacrificial death pertains only to the lives of the elite, the heroes, and it is one that some observers, like Robert Bellah, believe entered the national myth late, during the Civil War period.[11]

As with our reflection upon the future, the fundamental importance of dedication to the American dream is brought home to us by the unmistakable fact of its erosion and slipping away. In one area of national life after another, Margaret Mead's judgment seems to be borne out: the transmission of commitment has broken down. We might catalog the instances—the decline of interest in the armed forces, the unpopularity of the Indochina War, the decreasing interest in politics and the electoral process, the "dropping out" of minority group youth, as well as affluent middle-class young people. The Watergate hearings of 1973 were the occasion of lamentation by innocent and guilty alike over their discouragement of promising youth to "get involved" in the governmental system. In the last years, academic institutions reportedly show renewed interest in the theme of "human purpose," and foundations are willing to finance symposia and other projects devoted to the topic.

We turn again to Lincoln for a classic statement of what it is that we seem to be losing in these days, and his words in themselves press upon us by contrast with our times the urgency of our loss, suggesting to us that the gift of commitment to the future is indeed a manifestation of God's power in our midst. Lincoln spoke to the New Jersey Senate in February, 1861. He described the impact which stories of the battles of the American Revolution made upon him as a boy. "I recollect thinking then," spoke Lincoln, "boy even though I was, that there must have been something more than common that those men struggled for." This is the theme, a "more than common" future which elicited a struggle on the part of its servants. He goes on to say that his desire is that this struggle, which is for more than national independence, should continue. The struggle is really for a promise that "all the people of the world to all time to come" should share in. He continues:

> I am exceedingly anxious that this Union, the Constitution, and the liberties of the people shall be perpetuated in accordance with the original idea for which that struggle was made, and I shall be most happy indeed if I shall be an humble instrument in the hands

of the Almighty, and of this, his almost chosen people, for perpet-
uating the object of that great struggle.[12]

This is what the religious substance of our primal American myth
is all about.

The loss of the future and the loss of the ability to motivate and
mobilize oneself to sacrificial dedication go together. The sixties
and the seventies underscore the tenuousness with which they hang
on, the loss of which would destroy or alter decisively the very
being and identity of America.

SOMETHING MORE THAN THE AMERICAN DREAM

As the American dream itself is challenged and threatened in
our decade, the ultimacy to which it pointed and still may point,
the presence of God for America which it discloses, becomes all the
clearer to us. Although restoration of the authentic dream and its
power is certainly one part of the spiritual challenge that faces
Americans today, and even though we personally consider it dangerous to repudiate the dream out of hand, it would be a serious
misreading of our intentions to judge that we call simply for a
rehabilitation of the American traditions. That would be an inauthentic retrieval of American history.

Even though the heart of the primal myth is, at its best, a disclosure of God's power among us, it is also, in part, a betrayal of God
and a falsification of American experience. The very reality of the
identity crisis we spoke of in Chapter III is witness to this. The
disjunction between what we experienced in the sixties and the
dream is a testimony that our crisis today is grounded not only in
the disobedience and rebellion of evil or incompetent people
against the primal myth. The crisis would not have been averted if
only the symbols of our American identity had been polished more
brightly so that they could shine more luminously or if only we
had been more obedient to them. Over and above our attention to
the primal myth itself there comes into the discussion the question
of our *concealment* of elements of our past experience which did
not conform to the myth and which would have broadened and
amplified the myth. They were authentic witnesses to the truth,
struggling to come to the surface to unveil the truth for us, even if

we suppressed them. If our decade is in some sense a decade of trauma, defeat, and demoralization, it is so because, at least in part, the American dream at its very best is still inadequate and falsifying. The spiritual agenda of the American people includes restoration of its best traditions, but it also includes facing up to their inadequacies and reflecting on what new directions are called for in light of those inadequacies.

THE MISSING COVENANT

The covenant of belongingness is what is missing, and it constitutes a dimension that seems almost intrinsically unavailable to the American people. We are not the first to point to this particular missing dimension in our common life. Several recent commentators have lifted up this issue. The sense of belongingness within a covenant was part of both the early Puritan heritage of our nation and of the Enlightenment traditions that were especially strong among the Founding Fathers. For the Puritans, the covenant was a relationship of the community with the power and will of God which *preceded* the community's existence and its mandate to settle the new world. The Enlightenment thinking included a conviction that men thinking together could function harmoniously with the "laws of nature and nature's God." These two traditions, together, acknowledge a covenant in which man belongs to man, under the canopy of God's law and nature's law. There have been some suggestions that a recovery of these traditions can restore the sense of belonging that is needed in our national life. Richard Neuhaus calls for a recovery and expansion of this vision in an effort to sensitize us to what he calls the "seamless web of humanity," which involves a sense of responsibility for land, for the poor, for minorities.[13] Robert Bellah argues somewhat similarly, in a more cautious way, when he suggests that a critical appropriation of the Puritan vision may be a resource for building a genuinely communal ethic.[14]

However, neither the Puritan nor the Enlightenment traditions spoke effectively of covenant in the sense that we belong to each other and to the land, that our very existence as human beings is constituted by a responsibility to care for land and fellowman, just as we are cared for by both. The proof of the pudding is in the eating, which in this case means that what covenantal sense there was in earlier traditions did not promote a caring relationship for the land, the poor, or the Amerindian and black populations. On the contrary, as our description of the wreckage of the American past indicates, the athletic commitment of the straight arrows drove them on to new heights of development and exploitation. The depressingly small minorities who did care for the Indians, the blacks, and the land simply underscore how blind the American dream and its adherents were to the covenant of belonging and mutual caring. There was often a sense of the social character of existence, which produced the much-heralded American voluntary commitment to common causes—individualism is not the whole of the American past. But this corporate commitment is more a preference for team athletics over individual play than it is a recognition that we intrinsically belong to each other and must care for each other. Working together, an essential American trait, is not the same as caring for each other.

With respect to blacks, the Reconstruction period stands as the test whether the exclusion of blacks from the human ranks under the Founding Fathers was simply a pragmatic political decision that was necessary for long-term realization of the dream, or whether it was in fact a denial of the dream. The sad fate of the post-Civil War years, culminating in the northern Republican party's gradual growing indifference to the black population and in the Supreme Court's striking down civil rights legislation in 1883 and approving separation of the races in public accommodations in 1896, revealed that the nation did _not_ act as though the institution of slavery was contrary to the American dream. The nation as a whole did not concur with Lincoln that a future had been unleashed in the founding documents of our nation, a future that had to be carried forward in the Civil War period. The nation concealed once again the possibilities, the "might have beens," that were open to us. Lest we take too easy comfort in the opinion that the South was to blame for the Reconstruction events, let us recall that in his Dred Scott decision of 1857, Justice Taney based his opinion that blacks were not covered by the Constitution on a considerable amount of evidence that the discriminatory legislation in northern states bespoke a common opinion that blacks were never intended to share "rights and privileges, and rank, in the new political body throughout the Union...."[15]

What we have described in some detail here with regard to blacks can be extended to cover the appalling lack of a sense of caring responsibility toward Indians, women, the poor, or the land. The plain truth is that the symbols of American identity did not portray—nor did they implant in the hearts of Americans—a sense that the straight arrow of ascent was involved in a covenant of belonging.

In the preceding chapter, we concluded that three specific crises have been disclosed by the traumatic events of the past decade: the baring of our finitude and the loss of innocence that goes with that finitude, an identity crisis that is rooted in a basic symbolic impasse within our American myths, and the dilemma of resolving adequately the tension between freedom and control. We are now arguing that these crises are *not* simply the product of disobedience to these symbols. Rather, these crises are also rooted in intrinsic deficiencies in the symbols and in the concealments Americans perpetrated to cover over the disjunction between their symbols and their experience. The single-minded projection of the people, like a high-flying arrow, willing to discipline self and suffer hardships, whatever its admirable qualities, is sublimely innocent of the discreteness and finitude of existence and of the tightly woven network of relationships in which it must carry out its flight. Like the high-flying mythic figure of Icarus, whose too high ascent toward the sun resulted in disaster as the wax that bound the feathers in his wings melted, the primal myth of our identity is oblivious to the disaster that comes from overlooking the finite realities of our interrelatedness to land, minorities, and the poor. The Puritan images of the covenant with God have not helped us, because we were so sure that God was on our side. The checks and balances provided by our pragmatic and realistic Enlightenment forebears were not adequate brakes upon us, because the major parties and the three branches of our government did not check and balance each other vis-à-vis the myth. Only a sense of the covenant with land and fellowmen that implies reciprocal caring could keep our finitude before us so as to counter our invincible innocence. In other words, only an *alteration* of the myth can open Americans to the covenantal realities of our common life.

Similarly, the symbols of high-flying projection toward an open future coupled with boundless disciplined energies are peculiarly unable to provide the kind of symbolic response to error, defeat, and self-deception that can satisfy the spiritual needs of the American people in these years. Merely increasing the volume of the traditional message until it reaches fortissimo, and calling for a comparably increased dedication to the American dream will never deal adequately with our need to understand the disjunction we feel—how it came to pass and what it means for our American dream. The dream as such will never be able to help us in our current identity crisis. Finally, the primal myth cannot help us deal with the dilemma of control versus freedom that has come to the fore with increasing urgency in recent years. Icarus did not want controlled flight, he wanted height. He recognized no concrete interrelatedness between himself, the stuff of wax and feathers that enabled the flight, and the sun he aimed to reach. If he had, he would have understood the limits within which his flight could succeed. America, too, is spiritually geared to attain height. As long as our cockpit possesses only an altimeter and no gauges of belongingness, we have no chance to deal with the problem that is central for our future.

What is the Evil in American Life?

We spoke in Chapter III about the subtle and necessary relationship between evil and the disclosure of truth, in individual existence as well as in our national life. This truth was described as the truth about our finitude, about the identity confusion, and about the centrality of the need to balance our notion of freedom with a sense of belongingness. Furthermore, we come to see in what sense the encounter with evil is an experience of the sacred, because there was disclosed to us not only the painful truth of our sickness, but also the religious depths of our national existence. These religious depths come to our consciousness as we probe the ultimate dependencies of our national life and appreciate the sense in which the primal myth of our American identity has been a vehicle for expressing how God's power has been manifested under the relativities of the American experience: as the power of the future and of sacrificial commitment to it.

In other words, at this first level, evil was used in an almost neutral sense as *the occasion for reflection and the unveiling of truth for us.* In this chapter, we have definitely moved on to lift up a second dimension of evil. Now we have spoken of evil in a way that is certainly not neutral, but rather in a way that involves us more intimately. We have suggested that the mythic vehicles for holiness in our American life, despite their power, their integrity, and their precious character (and we mean to honor them in these respects) *can be instruments of evil at the very same time that they are bearers of God's power and means for our understanding of and participation in that power.*

Only the most ostrich-minded among us will want to deny the first face of evil. Who is so desensitized that he or she has not felt the shock waves of trauma roll through the body politic and the social organism of America since the heyday of Dwight David Eisenhower? But the second face of evil arouses different responses. It brings out the best or the very worst and most pathological in human beings. This is why we engage in concealment and self-deception regarding our history—recent history as well as far removed events. Here we are inclined, at first flush, to deny the evil, to attempt to ignore it, or to scapegoat, blame it on others, or to insist that *we* have not pushed the dream hard enough and far enough. We do nearly anything to avoid facing the almost intolerable truth that the symbols of holiness can also be vehicles of evil. The economic and human exploitation of the nineteenth century was not the consequence of intrinsic faults within the straight-arrow myth. Rather, it was a case of social Darwinism: God meant for the strongest to succeed, and if the strong had to reach the heights over the backs of those who could not compete so well or at the expense of despoiling the land and its resources, that must be destiny's plan. Such subterfuges are not uncommon to us.

There is no question but that one of the great spiritual problems that faces Americans today is to grasp how the symbols that bear holiness can also be instruments of evil. We have described the inadequacies of the conventional right, left, and center in order to show how widespread the voices are who present options that cannot possibly help America face up to its spiritual problem. It will require a spiritual reforming of the greatest magnitude to help the American people recognize that even a myth as true as the American dream wreaks evil because it is only part of the truth, not the whole truth. When a partial truth is pushed to its ultimate point, its truth is ironically transformed into its opposite, evil and the demonic. Its partialness can, in fact, when pushed too far bring the betrayal of even that partial truth. The fragility of the position in which the dream now stands stems from the fact that so many Americans either will not admit that partial truth can become evil or they will not grant that partial truth is still worthy of respect even after it has wrought evil. Can we understand that our very success as America is in a strange way the evil in American life? Can we understand that the sacred power which played into the emergence of the symbols of that success is no less holy for the evil in which its symbolic expressions became implicated? Can we face up to the reality of the wrath that inexorably pours out when men and women who are in touch with the holy pursue too relentlessly the partial vision of the holy which has been granted them? Can we believe that the people that has been through the fire of such wrath can retain its identity in a transformed way and yet follow the path of the holy that courses through the bloodstream of its life? These are the kinds of issues that America faces now.

The questions we have just raised are all focused on the one question, Can Americans come to understand the demonic element in their deepest aspirations and the symbols that express those aspirations in their national myth? The term *demonic* has been widely used and debased in recent years, particularly as the extreme critics of America have employed it (although, as we shall see, their use of the term is not without point). Demonic is not equivalent to perverse or satanic. We use demonic (as Paul Tillich did) to describe the relationship of evil to good.[16] The demonic never appears except in conjunction with the good, and it refers specifically to the drive inherent in the *concrete manifestations of goodness* to elevate themselves to unequivocal identity with their source, goodness itself. The demonic is the power that takes a manifestation of goodness and pushes it beyond its capabilities and its finiteness, so that the manifestation of goodness becomes transmuted into a vehicle of evil and destruction.

To say that something is demonic, therefore, is to acknowledge that it is basically good, but that its goodness has been nullified by its own pretensions to be more than a vehicle for goodness, to become *the Good*. The American dream has, as we have described, been a vehicle of goodness and holiness, a mode of God's presence among us. That dream has also become demonic, because it has been pushed beyond itself, and in the hands of Americans has become *the* Good and *the* Holy. The extreme critics have often failed to recognize that in calling America demonic, they were in fact speaking of a phenomenon that was a vehicle for goodness. And the chauvinists who reacted so bitterly against the charge of the demonic fell victim to the same ignorance.

When we say that the evil in American life has been the American dream itself, we are saying, in this profound way, that the dream is demonic. Like all vehicles of goodness and holiness, its adherents have lost sight of its finiteness, its character as a *vehicle*, and thereby they have decisively diminished its power for good.

THE AMERICAN CIVIL RELIGION

What we have considered throughout these reflections as the "American dream," the "American primal myth," or the "symbols of American identity" has been spoken of by scholars as the "religion of the republic" (a phrase utilized by Sidney Mead) and the "civil religion." The latter term, which was brought into prominence in 1967 by Robert Bellah, has become the central rubric under which to locate the religious dimension of American national life.[17] A considerable number of sociologists, historians, and theologians have, over the years, talked about the "sacred symbolism" of American society (Lloyd Warner), the "common religion" of our society (Robin Williams), or the religion of the "American way of life," but Mead and Bellah have probably stimulated the most discussion of the idea that there is a common, secular religion which has been significant for American common life since the beginning.[18] There has been a good deal of questioning Bellah's notion, for example, whether it really qualifies in the technical sense as a religion. There seems to be consensus, however, that we can indeed speak of what John Wilson calls "the common symbol-horizon of a social order," which, as Bellah suggests, defines "in broadest terms the nature of reality," a religious symbol system that provides stable points of reference for human action in a society[19]—a concept similar to what Cox calls "people's religion," as that "religion" touches national life.

For the past fifteen years, it has been popular for Christian theologians and critical nonreligious secularists to condemn the civil religion out of hand for its pretensions, its threat to Judaism and Christianity, and for the perversions it has spawned in American life. Some observers, like Sydney Ahlstrom in his recent *A Religious History of the American People*, have suggested that in any case, the civil religion with its basic symbols of identity is dead, a casualty of the 1960s.[20] We are more inclined to agree with Bellah that the battered and bruised symbols of the civil religion still live,[21] and we would add that they are the first and primary access to religious meaning and transcendent realities for most Americans.

Since the civil religion of America is the bearer of the symbols of identity that we have described, it shares the failures and trauma that we have spoken of. The American people are experiencing the dislocation that any religious group would experience when it is disclosed that their religion itself shares actively in evil. The bearer of transcendence and ultimacy is itself caught up in evil—that is a shaking experience that human beings can scarcely absorb without devastating consequences. Little wonder that Ahlstrom and others believe that the civil religion is dead, simply because the sixties laid bare its inadequacies. It is not surprising, when the experience of the past decade is put in these religious terms, that a counter-culture has arisen and has exemplified so fully what Ahlstrom suggests. If any further testimony is needed to indicate how difficult it is for men and women to weather a crisis in their religion, we reproduce here the reflections that Bellah received from a friend who was actively engaged in the presidential campaign of George McGovern in 1972:

Could it be that the old myths have run out? Could it be that there is so little power in the old myths left that they are no longer able either to preserve the old culture or inculcate a revolutionary step within old forms? Isn't the malaise that everyone feels today the result of the fact that old values no longer have meaning and no new ones have taken their place?

Maybe we don't need a second coming of Lincoln's new birth of freedom. Maybe that won't work any more. Maybe the answer is not to recreate the old myths in a more humane context. Maybe that can no longer be done. Maybe we have to go through a period of living an atonal cultural life where it is not clear where home base really is. Maybe the attempt of George McGovern and people like myself to humanize American culture within the present social framework will fail. What then? Do we really want a new Jefferson—who will not own slaves? Can we have him if we wish? Maybe we will be served only by something we have never seen before.[22]

Bellah's friend is working for a humanizing of American culture. We believe that reforming must accompany rehabilitation, since the old myths cannot be absolved, even in their most beautiful moments, from responsibility for the crisis we are in. We said earlier that America *will* respond to its crisis religiously, no matter how secular Americans may profess to be at times. But the religious response that will come most naturally to us will be that of the civil religion. We posed the question in terms of *not whether* America will respond religiously, but *how*; *not whether* there will be religion, but whether it will be *good* religion or *bad*. Ironically and tragically, even those high-minded, sensitive persons who call for a more humane reaffirmation of the best of American primal symbols are in danger of reinforcing bad religion in America unless their "humanizing" is in fact a code word for substantial reformation of those symbols.

If, then, the civil religion of America shares so fully in the failures of the American dream, if we can go so far as to label it "bad" religion and even "demonic," why not join forces with those who would dismiss it, proclaim its death, work hard to bury it? First of all, because the civil religion, despite its battering, is still the major opening to transcendence for most Americans, and the only one for many. Secondly, because the civil religion does bear the potential within itself of exercising a transcendent critique upon American performance and upon itself. And finally, because no social order can exist without a symbol system to guide it, it seems unlikely that the American symbol system of the next hundred years will be other than a reformed continuation of the civil religion that has functioned for the past three hundred years.

The mainline American tradition reflects a symbol of the future and its power and promise as a *transcendent future*. This understanding may be documented from our previous references to Lincoln and the Puritan traditions. It is underscored by the current rediscovery by American historians of the apocalyptic and millenialist Protestant streams that have flowed into the symbolism of the national life. The sometimes bizarre millenialist theology of American Protestants in the eighteenth and nineteenth centuries was quite successfully secularized, brought into conjunction with other traditions (like the Puritan) that emphasized the transcendence of the future which America pursued, and became a strong base for American self-understanding.[23] Richard Nixon, then Vice-President, enunciated this sense in a 1960 spech which included these words: American "rights to freedom, to independence, don't come from men, but come from God."[24] Or, as Bellah puts it: Civil religion points to a "religious dimension of American political life that has characterized our republic since its foundation, and whose most central tenet is that the nation is not an ultimate end in itself but stands under transcendent judgment and only has value insofar as it realizes, partially and fragmentarily at best, a 'higher law.' "[25] Bellah believes that the civil religion exercised its transcendent vision in the time of the colonialists to mobilize energies behind independence; during the Civil War period it dealt with the slavery issue and wrestled with the martyrdom of the soldiers and the President who fought against slavery. Today, Bellah believes we can see that the civil religion exercised transcendence in the form of "long-term pressure for the humane solution of our greatest domestic problem, the treatment of the Negro American."[26] What faces us, he believes, is the challenge of developing a communal ethic that will enable us to live responsibly in a revolutionary world. This new challenge will, he suggests, demand a universalizing of the civil religion and possibly the incorporation of hitherto "non-American" traditions, such as Japanese Buddhism and Navaho and Hopi Indian motifs.

Richard Neuhaus has argued for the transcendence of the civil religion in his documentation of the absence of religious invocations to justify the Indochina War. Both Lyndon Johnson and Richard Nixon knew from the public opinion polls that Americans would not give religious sanction to that war. The civil religion, in fact, conflicts directly with the war policies of the government, demonstrating that the civil religion is not identified with the *government* of the United States, but with the *people*.

> As the opinion polls turned against official policy, it became more obviously self-defeating to threaten a majority of the American people with excommunication from this nation community "under God." The Johnson and Nixon administrations both recognized that the language of morality, conscience, and divine purpose has been co-opted by the opposition; such language is, therefore, to be avoided, lest the protest be given greater legitimation.[27]

Since the civil religion and its myth are necessary for the American nation, Neuhaus's program calls for rejuvenating the religion in the direction of the renewal of the covenant themes that have been enunciated in the past, to mobilize the "American Empire" to care for the poor, the minorities, the hungry, the persecuted, and the alien. He spells this out thus:

> It is not enough for the churches to ride along in a legitimating capacity on the bandwagon of radical revolutionary thought because such thought, at least in its present forms, requires the repudiation of the American experience. America hardly needs increased guilt feelings or more reasons for despising itself. It does need a new understanding of itself in a historical dispensation in which its power can be an instrument for creative change. In short, the American civil religion needs to be updated and given a new articulation in order that this country can, not only avoid more Vietnams, but also "be a blessing to the nations of the earth." In the symbiotic relationship between American civil religion and explicit biblical religion, the churches have a bigger public service to perform than has been undertaken to date in the religious protest against the war in Vietnam.[28]

J. Earl Thompson has also issued such a call.[29]

Although we have expressed some small disagreement with Neuhaus's way of speaking about the revivifying of the civil religion, we agree that the kinds of insights that Bellah refers us to are simply overwhelming arguments to retain the primal American symbols. It is a distortion of the way human beings live their lives in society and history to believe that symbol systems just disappear, to be replaced by new ones overnight. It is in the interest of all Americans not to destroy or dismiss the civil religion but rather to work for its critical reformation and vivification.

The greatest service that Chrsitians may be able to perform for their fellow Americans today may be to help reform and thereby vivify their national religion. The blistering, one-sided critiques that Christian theologians aimed at the civil religion in the fifties and the early sixties must be replaced, just as the uncritical devotion of many other Christian preachers and lay people must be abandoned. The Christian task in the spiritual reforming of the American soul in the seventies and the eighties is one of correction and fulfillment of that soul's natural religion. This reforming and vivifying of the civil religion is probably the single most important element in defining America anew in our generation. We now turn to spelling out the forms that this strategy takes.

THE CHRISTIAN TASK—HERMENEUTICAL HONESTY AND THEOLOGICAL DIALOGUE

The Christian activity of reforming the civil religion, that is, helping to redefine America, falls into two aspects, one of which is chiefly a process, the other primarily a preoccupation with substantive religious meanings. We perceive the process to be the functioning of the Christian faith as a force for hermeneutical honesty. We mean that the Christian faith must be an instrument for the honest interpretation of American history. This function needs little elaboration here, because we described it in detail in Chapter III under the heading "Retrieving American History." Hermeneutical, or interpretational, honesty includes the insistence that the past be freed from the concealments and evasions of events that may be contrary to our hopes and desires, but which may nevertheless be unpleasant sources for understanding the truth of God's presence in our national existence. Interpretational honesty also includes the aim of reflecting on what the past might have been, what possibilities have been revealed in the past but not followed up and actualized. In this aspect of its activity, Christian faith must militate against all authoritarianism in historical interpretation, rejecting all claims to privilege, to secrecy, and to the ruling of some historical question out of bounds to critical historical study. Although we touch upon this activity only briefly here, we refer the reader to Chapter III, to recall the power and the possibility which interpretational honesty holds for American life.

There is no possibility for actualizing a more humane and ͘ ːa-cious future for America if we hide from ourselves the truth of the past. We form our identity as a people by casting forth our common life toward the possibilities that we foresee in the future. The future calls us, both as a power that burgeons within us and as an objective image that lures us from the outside. But the future toward which we move is not an ideal, fantasized future; it is the real future of the real people we are. The real America includes the thrusting, brawling Adam that massacred Indians, oppressed the blacks, ignored the poor and infirm, laid waste Indochina. This real past which makes up America just as surely as the high points and bright ideals that we affirmed, this past will be incorporated in our future. Our future is the future of the high-dreaming, yet Negro-repressing America. The future is not necessarily a nightmare because of the blots in our past, but it is *different*; furthermore, a future that pretends to overlook that America is forever racified, Vietnamized, as well as Puritanized and Jeffersonized, is an unreal, fanciful future that will be a demonic future, a nightmare. Honest understanding of our past is essential for future fulfillment and present peace—and the Christian faith must count this honesty as a high priority in America for its own work.

This work for historical honesty includes the peaceful uses of the past. True peace is both wholeness and healing, even though, unfortunately, not every truth-sayer in our midst recognizes this. How can the practice of historical honesty bring about the dialogue that is necessary in our movement toward the future fulfillment of our possibilities? This dialogue does not come automatically, although many muckrakers and debunkers seem to think it does. Historical honesty must be assimilated to a healing manner. This healing manner includes trauma and confrontation, since no individual or group hears gladly the truth about the past and the significance of that truth for the present. Here the psychotherapeutic model proves suggestive: The retrieved past is to be understood and internalized, and thus it is to provide the basis for a healthy thrust into future possibilities.

The oppressed must be inspired by the retrieval of the past to authentic responsibility; they must give up the tendency to scapegoat the past, a strategy that reinforces their victim image and thus immobilizes their future. They must confront their oppressors and yet they must be convinced that facing up to their past provides the basis for their proud, authentic best selves to be actualized. This is a task of spiritual formation of major dimensions. It requires nothing less than what Gandhi continually practiced in his confrontations of Satyagraha, in which he provided morale-with-critique for both the oppressed and the oppressor.

One of the problems of the sixties and the seventies is that the enormous amount of debunking historical revisionism is either simply lying unused or it is exploited in pathological ways. Whereas the black community, for example, has achieved considerable success—through enormous effort—in using the "new history" as a basis for building pride, weakening the victim-image, and redirecting hostility, other groups have done far less. There has been virtually no attempt to help the American victims of the Indochina War from the lower and middle classes, blacks and whites, to deal with the truth that the war was unnecessary, perfidious, and unwon. As a consequence, the considerable amount of what we now know about that war is still acting pathologically in its impact upon veterans, the injured, and their families. Until the history of the Indochina War becomes a force for healing, Americans will not be able to move forward authentically from their now forever Vietnamized past, just as the Germans have yet to reach the point where they can authentically move forward from their forever Nazified and de-Judaized past. The truth about the Vietnam experience cannot be released for healing among the victims until the movers of that history become strong enough to face the truth. The healing dialogue will come when the President, the generals, and the munitions producers can share the same room with the injured GI's, the widows, and parents of the dead and talk about the war honestly and project their futures together in honesty. Of course, somewhere along the line the Indochinese themselves will have to be heard.

It may be simplistic to invoke the biblical injunction to "speak the truth with love," but that ancient wisdom does capture the essence of the enormous task which the hermeneutical dimension of the current situation sets before us. It may be useful to remember that loves does not imply muting the consequences of the truth and that speaking the truth does not absolve one from entering into relationships with the hearers so that wholeness may grow among the persons involved. The Christian faith possesses the symbols that motivate a quest for truth; we believe that the truth is the most liberating power of all, inasmuch as God himself is Truth. These symbols form the basis for the Christian faith's involvement in the process of historical honesty. The Christian faith must devote itself to speaking the truth with love to America, particularly since so few other forces exist in our nation for this task.

The Christian faith is also concerned with theological substance. Redefining America demands that we engage in critical theological dialogue with the civil religion. Underlying our proposal for theological dialogue is the assumption that the civil religion is just what the term denotes—a *religion*. And if it is a religion, we suggest that a *religious response* to it is appropriate as one important strategy for its reforming. Such a strategy will not be able to accomplish some of the desired outcomes that an insightful sociological, economic, or psychological critique might bring to bear, but it has some possibilities that are not open to other modes of discourse. A religious response is, after all, meeting the civil religion on its own ground—something that the theological critics of the fifties and early sixties abhorred. The religious response to the American myth acknowledges that Christian faith and the American dream are cousins of a sort, members of the same family of intent, in that both *are* religions. Acknowledging the kinship does *not* mute criticism (the Christian theological understanding of the demonic character of religion—civil and Christian—is not a soft form of criticism!), but by doing so, we understand *from the inside*, so to speak, what reformation is about.

Inherent in our proposal for the dialogue with the American dream is the conviction that altering that dream and reforming it cannot be brought about by external critiques, emanating solely from social or economic theory. There must also be a *religious* component in the dialogue, because the civil religion will not transform itself into social or economic theory, even though its dogmas presuppose such theories. The theological dialogue we engage in here is in fact a doctrinal challenge to the civil religion which grows out of the encounter between two religious options—Americanism and Christianity. The premise is that *doctrinal alternatives* must be available in the pluralistic American marketplace, if the civil religion is to be reformed and vivified as we believe it must be.

THE ARENA OF THEOLOGICAL DIALOGUE

The theological dialogue of the Christian community with the civil religion of the American people will be carried out most naturally and profitably on themes that deal with the power of the future and the sacrificial dedication which that future requires. It is around these two main dogmas that the two religions intersect and diverge.

This combination of motifs—future and sacrifice—has recurred throughout our essay. It is no violation of the facts of recent history to observe that the loss of the American future and the cutting of the nerve of dedication to that future are what terrify us as a people today—not just an undifferentiated threat to our physical and cultural survival, but the loss of the future which the settlers of the land and the Founding Fathers laid down for us in the dream. The sacrificial motif is just as crucial, since the dream itself points to a *struggling* ascent toward the future, an ascent that requires sacrificial dedication. The reality of one motif involves the other, the loss of one weakens the other. The loss of these realities is terrifying to Americans, not because their loss deprives us of the opportunity to be heroic, but because it deprives us of what up to now has been the basis of the specific American identity.

We have taken the further leap of interpretation to say that these two motifs are of deepest religious import for our common life, that they are in fact symbolic vehicles for expressing the way in which the power of the Holy, God himself, has chosen to manifest himself among us in our distinctive and relative American situation.

If this were not the case, the loss of future and dedication to it would not terrify us so.

Finally, the future/sacrifice motifs are so central to the Christian faith that they form an opportunity for dialogue with the civil religion that will not pull the faith off its base and distort it from the outset. If our preceding analysis is correct, the same may be said for the civil religion. We believe that a reformed vision of the future/sacrifice realities can contribute to the spiritual regeneration of the people that is necessary if we are to renew ourselves in the midst of the dilemma that grows out of the revelations of our finitude, of our deep-seated identity crisis, and of our inability to deal with the problem of freedom and control. Now we turn to the dialogue itself to spell out the contentions we have just enumerated.

THE WRATH OF THE SIXTIES AND THE SEVENTIES

Christian faith can make an immediate contribution to the American sensibilities by focusing particularly upon the experience of the past decade's encounter with events of evil. It can do so, because it understands what it means for human beings and societies to experience wrath. In this, it can contribute both to a constructive interpretation of the past decade and also criticize the faulty interpretations of those who refuse to face up to the experiences of evil during these years. The Christian faith knows that wrath is the consequence of the frustration of God's will. God does not overrule man's freedom, and this accounts for the fact that, despite God's presence, human beings can effect great evil. But God does not shield men from the consequences of their actions. The thwarting of God's will is also, Christians believe, the frustrating of the essential human nature, so that a violation of God's will is a violation of human nature and destiny. In sum, the thwarting of God's will results inevitably in wrath which lessens both God and man.

Since we have taken such pains to identify the presence of God in American experience with the power of the future that is celebrated in the symbols of the American dream, we can say that wrath is a consequence of the thwarting of the future in American life. Christian theology has traditionally spoken of *deus revelatus*

(God revealed) and *deus absconditus* (the hidden God). The revealed God performs his "proper work" (*opus proprium*) and the hidden God performs work that is "alien" to his nature (*opus alienum*). The hidden God is the thwarted God and his alien work is wrath. He performs this work not because he is spiteful and jealous, but rather because he will not violate the freedom which is essential to the creation he has unleashed and will not shield men from the consequences of their actions. We may transform these theological categories into talk about the future and speak of a *futurus revelatus* and a *futurus absconditus*, as well as of the proper and the alien activity of the power of the future.

Thus, we can understand that the deprivation of the rights of blacks and other colored minorities was an evil from the first. The primal symbols of America, as embodied in the Declaration of Independence and the Constitution, revealed this evil to us, in that they spoke of a future that meant making actual the inalienable rights of life, liberty, and pursuit of happiness (property) that belonged to all human beings by virtue of their createdness. The failure to enact this revealed truth in the colonial period was itself a thwarting of the *futurus revelatus*. As Lincoln saw, the grounds for this violation of the vision of man's future may be perfectly understandable in pragmatic, political terms, and the colonialists were permitted to exercise their freedom as they thought necessary at the time. We might even conclude that they did correctly assess the pragmatic realities of their time. But the humanity repressed by their understandable pragmatic decisions and the energies represented by that humanity are as real as the decisions of the Founding Fathers. Furthermore, the pragmatic correctness of those men at that time cannot negate the natural consequences that must flow both from their correctness of judgment and from their repressiveness. This is what Lincoln understood more fully than most Americans of his day. With no thought of avoiding the wrath—indeed, he struggled valiantly to open his contemporaries' eyes to the fact that their woe was in fact a manifestation of wrath—he nevertheless believed that by rectifying the colonialists' deviation from the *futurus revelatus* further wrath might be avoided and the future might function through its proper work of enhancing freedom throughout the entire world. One might even go so far as to say

that, given the two hundred years of disabilities suffered by blacks
up to that time, what happened in the Reconstruction is all that
could reasonably be expected. We do *not* subscribe to this thesis at
all, but even if one did, one could hardly deny that that period represented little of the future fulfilled and obeyed; a consequence of
the future thwarted once again would mean more wrath—the kind
of wrath that came to a violent head in the sixties and continues
today. If the future is not allowed to perform its proper work, it
will perform nevertheless, but the form of that work will be an
alien one, a wrathful one.

The Christian recognizes one more essential aspect of the work
of God, namely, that wrath falls upon guilty and innocent alike.
The Christian recognizes human solidarity, but he might well
reject notions of "corporate guilt." The wrath that we have known
in these last ten years need not be ascribed to the fact that every
last American is guilty of racism or militarism or imperialism or
sexism or capitalist exploitationism. Wrath of the future-thwarted
knows no distinctions. The poor have always known this. The black
or white man who died in Vietnam simply because he was poor
and unable to get an academic deferment may have been neither
imperialist nor militarist, but he felt the wrath of the future of the
American dream thwarted. The middle-class white family who
complains that the deterioration of the inner-city schools is ruining
the future of their children need not have deserved that fate
because of their own particular racist tendencies. No, these persons
may be fully innocent of racism, but that does not preserve them
from the wrath of the *futurus absconditus*. If the power of the
future is the power of God in our midst (and also, therefore, the
power of man's essential nature), it cannot be thwarted with
impunity. That future will not be content with human efforts to
manipulate it in distorting ways. It will not be restricted to any
group or class. That power of the future will destroy the attempts
to thwart it, and its destruction will strike innocent and guilty
alike.

This insight of the Christian faith may seem to be a gospel of
bad news, but in the long run it is in fact a message of good news,
in the same way that the potter's wheel of Jeremiah or the surgeon's cutting scalpel may be understood as instruments of creativ-

ity and healing. Lincoln, for example, was by no means immobilized by his understanding of the wrath that attended white America's treatment of blacks. He was caught in no cul-de-sac because of his sharp vision of wrath. On the contrary, his insight enabled him to set a course of action, which, although it went against the grain of his own personal opinion that blacks were inferior, was so positive and so vast that it overwhelmed his fellow countrymen, outstripped their energies and their imaginations. Similarly, the Christian message of the future's wrath opens up avenues for dealing with the basic problems that confront us. It is a sad mistake to label the Christian preaching of wrath as "bad-mouthing" America —as unfortunate as it would be to charge the surgeon with assault and intent to kill.

Quite to the contrary, the clearheaded sense of the wrath which attends the future-thwarted criticizes and calls into question those more soothing strategies that do in fact close off avenues of dealing with our problems. Scapegoating must be placed near the top of the list of strategies that ignore the realities of wrath. Americans have shared with most nations on earth the pattern of taking the people's eyes off the reality of wrath in their midst by invoking alien plots as the cause of national misfortune. Catholics, Jews, clergy, Communists, the yellow menace, black laziness, the malingering of the poor—all these and more have been alluded to many times in our history to account for America's difficulties. Most of them have been raised in the last decade to account for our national trauma. These paranoid, conspiratorial responses have in fact blocked America's progress toward the future, because they have at the same time diverted us from real issues, depleted our resources, and brought unnecessary retribution upon innocent segments of the population.

An understanding of wrath is healthier, we would argue, than strategies of scapegoating and other illusionary fantasizing. A keen sense of wrath is part of a sure defense against illusion. These strategies generally emanate from the right. It is also healthier than the strategies of the left that rely on the vague concept of "corporate guilt." This concept directs action toward the self, toward human beings, in a destructive manner, if it does not eventuate in utter despair. It is an almost primitive insistence that for every evil suffered there must be an occasion of guilt. This primitivism simply will not wash. It seems to us healthier (and therefore truer) to understand that even the innocent suffer wrath. Our task is not to wreak further vengeance against human beings as such, but rather to plot courses of action which—even though they cannot avoid the legacy of wrath that has built up for generations —can be mid-course corrections that may redress errors and possibly lessen the accumulation of future wrath.

When Christian faith insists that the civil religion of America attend to the reality of God's (or the future's) wrath, it is erecting a significant barrier to idolatrous pretensions that often beset the American dream. Earlier we spoke of the demonic character of the dream and its religion. The message of God's wrath underscores that finite forms reap only the whirlwind when they attempt to forget their finitude and usurp the position of the ultimate. An awareness of wrath, in other words, keeps the civil religion honest and defies its egregious claims. In this, the civil religion is no different from other finite vehicles that attempt to claim ultimacy for themselves. The Christian faith itself has often fallen victim to the demonic in the same way. For this very reason, and on the basis of the prophetic tradition in Judaism and Christianity that has always pricked the bubble of such pretensions, Christian faith sees with particular clarity the vulnerability of the civil religion to claim more for itself than it ought. The continued emphasis on the transcendence of the Holy over all its concrete forms is the best safeguard against demonic idolatries. Pointing to the wrath of God (or the future) is one necessary way of recalling us to God's transcendence.

EVIL, WRATH, AND SACRIFICIAL DEDICATION

Besides contributing to the American spiritual reformation through its understanding of wrath, the Christian faith also contributes quite different concepts of future and sacrificial dedication to the discussion with the civil religion. The motifs of future and sacrifice are as central to the Christian faith as they are to the American civil religion, but they are by no means identical, and in the elaboration of the differences, the Christian role in the current spiritual struggle becomes clearer. The Christian faith relates future and sacrifice in a comprehensive and complex manner. We believe that this Christian vision is relevant to the current American situation, but before we summarize it, we shall turn our attention to specific components of the Christian proposition, elaborating them in piecemeal fashion and then close with a fuller, more comprehensive statement. We turn first to the Christian understanding of sacrificial dedication, since it is intimately related to the reality of wrath that we have just reflected upon.

The Christian concept of sacrificial dedication differs in several important respects from the athleticism and martydom with which the American dream invests the concept. The central paradigm of sacrificial dedication for Christians is, of course, Jesus Christ, whose sacrifice is extended to all his followers in the manner that St. Paul expressed when he wrote in the twelfth chapter of his letter to the Romans: "Therefore, my brothers, I implore you by God's mercy to offer your very selves to him: a living sacrifice, dedicated and fit for his acceptance, the worship offered by mind and heart" (NEB). He wrote similarly in his second letter to the Corinthians:

> We are no better than pots of earthenware to contain this treasure, and this proves that such transcendent power does not come from us, but is God's alone. Hard-pressed on every side, we are never hemmed in; bewildered, we are never at our wits' end; hunted, we are never abandoned to our fate; struck down, we are not left to die. Wherever we go we carry death with us in our body, the death that Jesus died, that in this body also life may reveal itself, the life that Jesus lives. For continually, while still alive, we are being surrendered into the hands of death, for Jesus' sake, so that the life of Jesus also may be revealed in this mortal body of ours. Thus death is at work in us, and life in you. (NEB).

Although the sacrificial life to which Christians are called is a hard-fought struggling (Paul himself uses the imagery of the athlete disciplining himself) and even though many Christians seem to have equated sacrifice with martyrdom (and many have courted martyrdom eagerly down through the centuries), these two aspects of it are only a small part of the total concept for Christians.

The full Christian concept of sacrifice may be detailed in three aspects.[30] The action of sacrifice is (1) a declaration of the human actor's identity, but at the same time a confession that God is acting through the human deed; (2) the sacrifice is a response to evil, and the sacrifice is understood as an occasion (not cause) for grace to transmute evil's wrath into redemptive possibilities; (3) the sacrifice is undertaken within a network of consciously acknowledged interrelationships. The first of these characteristics is one that the American civil religion could endorse fully, and which it incorporates in its own understanding (whether a borrowing from the Christian tradition or not, we do not presume to say). The tradition of sacrifice in the Jewish as well as in the Christian scriptures emphasizes that it is God who is the ultimate actor in the sacrifice—whether that sacrifice be an offering of grain or of an animal, or of one's own disciplined and faithful life. The American tradition has rarely fallen for the widespread Christian perversion of sacrifice which views it as God's call for human beings to be self-effacing doormats, who in sacrificing themselves invite destruction. The biblical traditions do not sustain such a perversion. Sacrificial action in the New Testament, as well as for the prophet Isaiah's Suffering Servant, is that of an intentional, strong person, who sacrifices in order to fulfill a mission, not because of any masochistic desire for obliteration or for any false altruism. The essential concept of sacrifice entails a sense of a strong action simultaneous with a sense for being acted upon by the transcendent power of God. The sacrifice is what it is precisely because in its action God and human self come together, each retaining its integrity and wholeness.

One of the most fundamental differences between the sacrifice of the American civil religion and that of the Christian religion is that whereas the former conceives of sacrificial living as primarily an engine powering the flight of the straight arrows toward their heights (or as the martyrdom that befalls heroes), the Christian faith understands sacrifice as a response to evil. Here the differences are as great as those between night and day. The difference is expressed in the words of St. Paul that we just quoted: "Wherever we go we carry death with us in our body, the death that Jesus died, that in this body also life may reveal itself, the life that Jesus lives." The Christian engages in the sacrificial life because he believes that the sacrifice may be the occasion for a gracious, redemptive resolution of the wrathful conditions in which he exists. The cultic practices of the Hebrews and the death of Jesus stand behind this Christian conviction. The practice set forth in the Jewish scriptures seems to be that, in times of sin and evil, the sacrifice was brought to the priest, not in the hope of "buying off" God and bringing his favor, but rather in the belief that, by bringing an appropriate offering, the person or persons at the altar would be in a proper situation to receive whatever gracious resolution God would send. Sacrifice was also brought on the occasion of making an oath, renewing a covenant, seeking reconciliation with one's fellow human beings, and at times of giving thanks and rejoicing. The latter instances do not necessarily involve evil, but in all cases the hope was the same, that the sacrifice could be an occasion for God's grace. The sacrifice did not guarantee grace, it did not *cause* it or manipulate God. The active stance of man in bringing the offering provided that man would be an active participant in God's action. The grace bestowed by God was a participatory grace, not one in which the recipients were passive spectators.

The extension of this sacrificial notion to Isaiah's mythic Suffering Servant and to Jesus of Nazareth and his followers is a deepening of the concept. A person's very life may become the occasion of God's grace to resolve the wrathful conditions in which we live. In a mysterious manner that Christians know they can neither manipulate nor understand, the living sacrifice may be the occasion for the transmuting of wrath into redemptive possibilities.

The differences between the American civil religion and the Christian religion at this point stand out starkly. The athleticism of the American straight arrows tends to overlook the very conditions that rebound in wrath. The dedication that brings man from rags to riches dares life to lash back in wrath against the dedicated hero. The Christian faith sees sacrificial dedication as an acknowledgment that wrath is unavoidable just because of the blind arrogance of the straight arrows. The religious call of Christian faith to men and women is not that they should relinquish their integrity or their desire to achieve, but rather that they should understand that the greatest achievement is to die the death that Jesus died so that life may reveal itself, the life that Jesus lives. It is not a message which all Americans will accept, rather it is a vision that Christian faith proclaims for those who can reconcile it with their selfhood.

The Christian concept of sacrificial dedication is also a significant force for expanding the horizons of self-interest. The danger latent within the civil religion, and another element of its potential and actual demonic character, is that its vision is too often coterminous with a narrowly defined national self-interest. Consistently, throughout our history, for example, Americans have perceived that their mission was in behalf of all mankind, but they have interpreted that mission in terms so congruent with America's narrow economic, political, and military goals that no dimension of self-transcendence remained. In an ironic way, the nationalization of the American civil religion violates the basic assumptions of that civil religion itself, since it claims to be a vehicle of a vertical (that is, God's) as well as horizontal (that is, mankind's) transcendence. The Christian concept of sacrifice, in its emphasis that one suffers in behalf of all and for the fulfillment of all, militates against this nationalization. The Christian concept includes the notion that a person or a group (or a nation, as in the case of Israel) may even renounce its narrow interests and suffer privation in behalf of others. This might mean that the middle and upper classes allow the lower classes and minority groups compensatory treatment. It might dictate a lowering of the North American standard of living for the sake of an increase for those south of the equator. Such suffering and transformation of self-interest can hardly appeal very widely to the general populace, but it is an important critique and counter-reality for a civil religion that would demonically identify its divine revelation with narrow nationalistic goals. In the current American setting, the Christian concept of sacrifice stands as a religious call to a higher way, and as a critique upon the American dream of sacrificial dedication, contrasting the life-denial of a Saturn rocket engine with the agency of life and reconciliation that St. Paul describes and which Jesus Christ embodied.

The Saturn space rocket engine is not a bad analogy. The engine exists to defy basic interrelationships. It is built precisely as an agent for breaking out of the relationships created by gravity, so that man can shoot outside the orbit of his world and reach new frontiers. The Christian concept of sacrifice bears within it a fundamental acknowledgment of interrelationships. This acknowledgment is revealed in many layers of symbolism. In the earlier cultic rites, the sacrifice needed an earthy object—the best fruit of the harvest or the finest animal in the flock. Thus, symbolically and literally, nature and the land were related to the sacrificing human being. He used nature for his sacrifice, and his sacrifice was impossible without the natural offering. He was also caught up in a web of human relationships for his sacrifice. When the priest judged the fruit or animal to be worthy, he was judging the man also. The priest was always necessary. Oftentimes the sacrifice was a meal, eaten with family, friends, or with those whose reconciliation was wanted. Jesus' sacrifice included his final supper with his closest friends.

The sacrifice has a particular association in Jewish and Christian faiths with the covenant between man and God and between man and his society. *The* covenant was the covenant which God made with his people Israel. He chose this nation as his elect. This meant that every Israelite depended for his existence upon God and the chosen nation of his brothers and sisters. To be apart from God meant to be a no-body, a no-person. To be alienated from fellow Israelites was also to be a no-person, a nothing. The sacrificial rite became a regular ritual for celebrating this covenant of belongingness to God and people and for renewing it. Not all sacrifices were of this type, but this form became one of the central sacrifices. In preparing for his sacrifice, Jesus said at his final meal with his friends that the bread and wine were his body and his blood, and that both were a new covenant for the forgiveness of sins for all people. The earthly nature was there: bread, wine, body, blood. They expressed belongingness to God and the covenant of interrelatedness with the entire human community. Jesus raised to a higher power what Jews before him and Christians after him embody in their sacrifices. Selfhood is not relinquished, nor is ambition nor achievement (Jesus was, after all, fulfilling his manhood in his career, he was not a pathetic victim of circumstance). Rather, selfhood, ambition, and achievement are transformed, in intention at least, in an action which achieves and fulfills selfhood in concert with the natural order and the larger human community, under the divine presence and as an expression of the divine presence. In the sacrificial act, therefore, the Christian acknowledges and declares an identity radically different from the American straight arrow.

Significantly, the most important sacrificial offering in Israel was the peace-offering, the shalom offering. Shalom (peace) means belonging, belonging in wholeness to oneself, belonging to God and one's fellows. The greeting, "Shalom," means "May you belong this day, to yourself, to your God, and to your people, because then you will know peace, the peace of the covenant." The Christian faith asserts that wrath is transformed in the sacrificial dedication of men and women who perform the living sacrifice of the shalom and thus become shalom in the world. When Christian faith carries on its dialogue with the civil religion of America, it acknowledges an immediate bond with the American dream, since both are concerned with sacrificial living, but it calls the civil religion to reform its dedication into a form that may be more productive of genuine peace, shalom with man and nature. It lays bare the demonic character of the high-flying straight arrows' athleticism, and it also points to a better option. The Christian faith makes this contribution to the dialogue by placing its own concept of sacrificial dedication into the marketplace of ideas and actions. Its understanding of sacrifice will call into question very sharply the Saturn engine of dedication that has occupied the civil religon; it is only through that challenging, that calling into question, that shalom has a chance.

SACRIFICE AND FUTURE

The covenant peace of shalom which is God's fundamental gift and will for man is intimately related to the Christian understanding of future. The future is the manifestation, par excellence, of God's power and presence, according to Christian faith. In the New Testament, the embodiment of the future is the Kingdom of God and the agent of that future on earth is the Son of Man, the Messiah, the chosen and anointed one of God—for Christians, that is, Jesus of Nazareth who is the Christ (the anointed Messiah). Jesus came preaching a message of the Kingdom of God. In Chapter 15 of his first letter to the Corinthians, St. Paul interprets his resurrection as the first fruits of a harvest that would include all people and the entire creation. This message is a witness that what is really important for the world is not what has been but rather what will happen, not what we have been, but what we will become. As Father Teilhard de Chardin and others have asserted, the future holds the key for our basic nature, because what we shall finally be tells us who we are.[31] Secularly, the German philosopher Martin Heidegger expressed this by saying that man is made as the creature who is always acting so as to fulfill his future.[32] A whole generation of contemporary theologians, led by Wolfhart Pannenberg, has recovered this truth.[33] Christian faith can put such a premium upon the future because it is the premier manifestation of God's presence in our world.

In this, Christian faith begins at the same place that the civil religion does, and probably we have to do here with a direct borrowing, in which the American religion took over the Christianity of its first settlers and ideologues. It is no accident that America could accept and secularize the millenialist versions of the Kingdom. Again, as we observed with respect to sacrifice, the common starting point, however, cannot hide the considerable difference between the two religions. Since future is so important to both, it is essential that the Christian faith emphasize strongly the distinctiveness of its concept of the future, else its dialogue with America will be aborted from the outset.

For Christians, the understanding of the future is bound up with what is called the *apocalyptic* world view. We may simplify the scholarly details by the following description. In the apocalyptic vision, God is moving the created order toward the consummation and fulfillment which is his own will and fulfillment. This consummation entails the battle between good and evil and the conquest of the latter. In his hands he moves the entire created order toward the future he has prepared for it—the entire cosmos, human beings and nature, worldly history as well as Christian history, outer space as well as planet earth. By definition, the future cannot be disclosed before the end of time, because it *is* future. But God does send his agent to embody in advance a foretaste of the future—a foretaste that is a reliable indicator of what the future (and therefore essential) destiny of the cosmos is. In other words, he reveals *proleptically* what the nature of things *will be* (and therefore what that nature *is*). This is what the Pauline image of the first fruits is all about. The first fruits is not the entire harvest, nor is it identical to what the final harvest will be, but it is part of the harvest, and the finest part. Moreover, its appearance means that the harvest *has* begun, no matter how long the entire operation drags out.

This future is God's power and presence manifesting itself among us. It is a transcendent reality, since it is after all God himself. It calls into question all that exists on earth, since all earthly works and institutions will have to bow before the harvester and will be judged by their congruence with *the* future which is the final fulfillment of all things. History *will* be judged; it is not forever destined to continue as it is now going. But the Christian faith does not conceive of this future as too transcendent to involve man meaningfully, and that includes man in his freedom. Its basic view of God as being an involved God who has erected a covenant with his creation and who works for the wholeness or shalom of his people would not be compatible with a view of transcendence which excluded human beings or obliterated them. Humankind is meant to share in this onrushing future that defines the essential nature of man and the world. The example of the divine agent himself, Jesus of Nazareth, discloses what the form of human participation in the future is like. And that form is the form of sacrifice. It is impossible to speak of the thrust toward the divine future apart from the modality under which that destiny is present in our world, namely, the modality of suffering and sacrificial death, as we spoke of that sacrifice in the preceding section.

This means that sacrifice is not an end in itself. It is not a strategy of suffering for its own sake. It does not bespeak a negative or pessimistic view of life. Rather, it is the mode by which we grasp the future. Or, in other words, it is the mode by which the future grasps human beings and transmutes wrath into redemption. This, in a nutshell, is the Christian proposal to the world, particularly, in this case, to America and the American civil religion. We believe that this Christian vision is portrayed in succinct form in the eighth chapter of the Gospel of Mark. (Again, we simplify the critical, scholarly issues of interpretation.) Jesus has fed the multitude, and this raises questions concerning who he is. The Jewish leaders are cast as blind and unperceptive, as, later on, the disciples are, too. When Jesus gets to the disciples he asks who they say he is. Peter responds, "You are the Messiah." Jesus then proceeds to describe what must be the actions of the Messiah, namely, to go up to Jerusalem and die, only to rise again. The New English Bible has it: "He spoke about it plainly." Peter was so offended by Jesus that he "took him by the arm and began to rebuke him." But Jesus turned round, and, looking at his disciples, rebuked Peter. " 'Away with you, Satan,' he said; 'you think as men think, not as God thinks.' " Jesus then proceeds to describe the actions of those who would wish to follow him. "Then he called the people to him, as well as his disciples, and said to them, 'Anyone who wishes to be a follower of mine must leave self behind; he must take up his cross, and come with me.' "

What the biblical writer has to say in this section is significant, and, we believe, an epitome of the entire Christian vision. Many persons did not recognize who Jesus was, but some did believe he was the Messiah, the agent of the apocalyptically conceived future. These, however, did not conceive of the Messiah as a suffering figure, just as the Hebrews centuries before had not wanted to accept that the chosen one of Yahweh would take the form of the Suffering Servant described by Isaiah. The tension between the concepts of Messiah and suffering was so great that even Peter, leader of the disciples, is described as physically laying hold of Jesus in dismay or anger, and Jesus lashes back to hurl the epithet "Satan" at Peter. We know that several groups in Palestine are only too happy to accept a Messiah, but they did not expect him to suffer and die. Rather, they expected him to grab the future as it came round and swing with it, defeating evil and taking them with him. Jesus has to tell them the plain truth by his life, that suffering and dying, by definition, precede resurrection, that the future is appropriated and becomes real in and through the sacrificial act.

Here again, the divergence from the American primal myth becomes clear. The future is a future that incorporates for Chris-tians, by definition, the entire cosmos, earth, land, people in a cove-nant community, all of world history as well as the history of the elect ones. (This is intrinsic to the apocalyptic vision.) The transcendent and glorious dimensions of the future are shared by the American civil religion. But the belongingness of cosmos, land, *all* people, and *all* history together is more than the civil religion can comprehend, except in a few rare moments. The element of sacrifice is almost totally unavailable to the American understanding of future, except in its athletic version. We keep in mind what we said earlier about sacrifice, namely, that it is a reconciling action that aims at the wholeness of nature and the human community. To act for the future is, then, to act in such a way that one seeks the fulfillment of all—nature and humankind—in the context of one's own integrity and selfhood. This concept of future is almost totally at odds with the image of rocketing out of the relationships of earth and jettisoning behind the machinery that enabled the initial thrust—just as it is opposed to all of the images of advance over the wreckage that is left behind by the straight arrows. It is the wholeness of the future of the entire created order and its history that Christian faith wants to affirm.

The Christian concept of the Kingdom of God, since it is linked to the apocalyptic view and to the understanding of the future we have described, is markedly different from the American tradition. That tradition secularized the Christian view and made the Kingdom synonymous with empire. As such, it undergirded nationalistic drives for expansion—first geographical, later cultural and economic. For the civil religion, then, although the Kingdom is not always territorial. it *is* a concept of possession and imperial outreach. The future, necessarily, is the open dimension of time and space to expand this empire. The Christian doctrine, to the contrary, understands the Kingdom as God's power, his rule, which unfolds the destiny of his entire creation and which involves human participation. It is not something we possess or that we expand. Neither can it be identified with our personal or corporate goals. Rather, the Kingdom is a critical concept when contrasted to human pretensions, since it originates in God and is always unfinished in character. Americans could identify their goals with the Kingdom of God only by domesticating God—a thrust that is intrinsically contradictory of the very notion of the Kingdom of God apocalyptically conceived, since the Kingdom is by definition supranational and even supracosmic. The Kingdom of God and the future, then, take their place alongside the concepts of wrath and sacrifice both as constructive concepts and as brakes to the egregious pretensions of American nationalism.

DIALOGUE AMID THE CURRENT TRAUMA

If we were to summarize the Christian contribution to the dialogue with the civil religion of America as we have set forth the components in the preceding pages, we would have to put it thus: The Christian faith insists that we must attend in our common life (1) to the reality of the wrath of a future-thwarted and (2) to the character of the future itself as the thrust toward the wholeness or shalom of the entire natural and human community, which manifests itself in actions of dedication which embody that shalom, such actions being so constituted that they can only be called actions of sacrifice.

Christians do not expect that all, or even very many, Americans will accept these affirmations or put them into practice. But they do expect that they can exert a constructive influence by criticizing the civil religion of the people and its basic symbols and reminding the people that those symbols are in need of fundamental reform. In so doing Christians participate in the common American religious task of defining ourselves as a nation.

The Christian communities within the churches may play a role for Americans, if they can reform themselves to become demonstration communities where the future is honored and shalom is celebrated. Since the spiritual regeneration required of America is so great, individuals will be able to undergo reformation only if they are very strong and self-confident. For many Americans this strength and confidence will be available only through participation in supportive and stimulating new communities. The Christian churches, if they can in fact become such communities, may perform a service to Americans they attract. Most of these Americans will not be new converts, but rather "lapsed" Christians. In our view, it would be folly for the churches to entertain the strategy of serving America by converting its citizens—not only folly but probably demonic. Rather, the churches must cast their doctrines in the pluralistic marketplace of ideas, in creative and confrontational *religious* dialogue with the civil religion. This dialogue will be enhanced if the churches themselves exist as communities of identity commensurate with their doctrines and, as such, attractive even to those who will never join them.

We do not presume to be able to make specific proposals for dealing with each of the crises that we have outlined in the preceding pages. We intend to set forth the religious dynamic which may be useful to Americans as they work out our future in concrete ways in the years ahead.

WRATH AND THE AMERICAN IDENTITY CRISIS

In Chapter III, we described one of the key issues that has been laid bare by the trauma of the past decade as an identity crisis. What this decade has lifted up is the actual experience of error, failure, and self-deception in American life, and the symbols of the American identity do not allow for the incorporation of such negative experience into our system of meaning. If a redefinition of America is to be made, a redefinition that can grasp the people of America and give them wholeness as citizens, a way must be found to account for error, failure, and self-deception besides the conventional ways of discrediting those who point to such elements in our life. We have records aplenty of such persons being labeled as traitors, "bad-mouthing America," being associated with unfriendly foreign powers. The sixties have brought home the fact that if acknowledging these negative elements in America is bad-mouthing America, the experience of a large number of Americans, perhaps even a majority, makes them, too, traitors.

What we propose is that American public symbols must be stretched to the point where they can account for the fact that perfectly loyal and well-meaning Americans (as well as scoundrels in our midst) can betray the vision of the future that is in fact a signal of God's presence and power in our midst. And when that future is, for whatever reason, betrayed or thwarted, then wrath is the consequence—a wrath that falls upon guilty and innocent alike. Some such symbolism has often been held by the Christian churches in America, and Abraham Lincoln in his memorable second inaugural speech tried to introduce the symbol of wrath into the civil religion. It is embedded in our American bloodstream if we wish to capitalize upon it. But it has not become a

major motif. Perhaps there is no clearer example of our unwilling-
ness to incorporate wrath into our identity symbols than the regular
practice of the Presidents during the Indochina War to launch
attacks on their critics during the ceremonies in which they gave
Medals of Honor to widows of fallen servicemen. The Presidents
could not invoke the American God against their critics, but they
could accuse them of betraying the trust of those who died in the
war. There was an absolute inability to acknowledge that the
deaths could be the consequence of the wrath unleashed by a future
(both at home and abroad) that was thwarted by our policies in
Southeast Asia. It was only a rare spirit, like Lincoln, who could
honor the Founding Fathers and also acknowledge their reneging
on the dream, who could honor the southern states of the Union
and still say to them that the devastation they were absorbing was
the wrath of a just God.

Lincoln's healthy-mindedness needs urgently to be brought more
forcefully into our national religion, both his keen sense for the
wrath that accompanies disloyalty to our future and also respect for
the situations of those who thwarted the future by their actions.
We must find ways to give symbolic expression to our admission
of fallibility. Only thus will we be able to close the gap between
experience and symbols in our American life in a way that does
justice to our experience and still permits us to be fully American.
American Christians can contribute to this reformation of our
primal myth, if, as Daniel Berrigan recently said, they demonstrate
that their critique of America and their message of wrath is rooted
in loyalty to the American experience and not in fundamental
antagonism to it. He is quoted as saying, "In my sympathy with
liberation struggles elsewhere, I never forget that I am an American and a Christian. I want to be as indigenous to my culture as
they are to theirs."[34]

THE COVENANT AND AMERICAN FINITUDE

A second major issue uncovered by the events of the last decade
is a renewed disclosure that America does have limits—geographical, racial, economic, political. A great deal of what has been demonstrated to be destructive and evil in our national life stems from
our insistence that we are privileged to live as if there will be no

tomorrow, as if the treasury of good fortune is boundless, as if the chips would never be called in on our recklessness and abandon. We have spoken at length about the revelation of the concrete web of finite interrelatedness that has taken place in recent developments between the races and the sexes in our society and which looms ahead in relationships between the affluent North American societies and the "have-not" nations south of the Equator. Only the recognition of the covenant of belongingness can redress our blindness to our finitude. The flight of the straight arrows must not be canceled out altogether, but must be decisively altered, so that the ascent is reconciled with the covenant of reciprocal caring for each other that is central to our lives, even if we have not recognized it.

THE COVENANT OF SHALOM AND THE DILEMMA OF FREEDOM AND CONTROL

What we have sketched briefly as a response to the American denial of finitude is also relevant to the dilemma of freedom and control that we analyzed in Chapter III. There we outlined the need for control of private corporate ascent. Without new kinds of ways of shaping the future, the competitive impulses in our free enterprise system may well destroy the sustaining structures of belonging upon which we depend. On the other hand, we emphasized that the free initiative inherent in the American myth and tradition must not be forsaken for some centralized scheme of control. The leftist solution to the dilemma opts for a centralized control, negating freedom. The rightist response does not admit the need for control. The centrist position hopes that out of the continued interplay of free, competitive groups—checked by traditional means of limitation—we will be able to survive.

But if our analysis in Chapter III is correct, the dilemma cannot be evaded so easily. The contradictions simply will not go away. The thrust of our voluntarist society must be guided and shaped. But it must be done without sacrificing the liberties and initiating impulses of the American tradition. In some fashion we must find ways of being comprehensively intentional toward the future and at the same time remaining free. By "comprehensive" we mean fully conscious of our interdependence as nations, individuals, groups, in relation to each other and as living beings in relation to nature. Decisions must be made in the light of the effects they will have on this interdependence. "Intentional" means conscious choices about national priorities and directions. Only such intentionality in shaping our history can avert social and ecological disaster.

But how to get to "comprehensive intentionality" and yet remain free? One thing is certain, new thought about the theoretical and practical relation of freedom and control is necessary. John Raines has called for such an inquiry into the relation of freedom and control.

> In short, I refer to the whole thickness and matrix of the shared and everyday world, the simple truth of our common exposure before life and consequent ineluctable reliance upon one another. This is the fundamental dimension of man's ordering of his existence, and to it the marketplace negotiations of interest and power remain second-level realities—able to disrupt but not able to create or survive without. The interest-group/marketplace metaphor of society fails because it is theoretically incapable of finding an interpretive place for the realities of community and of the common good that lie at the root of man's collective existence.
>
> Moreover, there is a dimension here that extends beyond the issue of human cohesiveness at its everyday level to what we might call *the policy of public significance.* It has to do with man's investing the common life with his energy and attention, with his desire "to be public" and share in that reciprocal gratitude of civilization. Wilson Carey McWilliams is one of the few social scientists who addresses himself to this dimension of political reality. He puts it well when he says:
>
>> Modern America, with its liberal heritage, has thought of man's estate as a matter of property, something he comes into only when he makes things a part of him as the things he controls: his *owing* is a stronger and truer source of dignity than *owning.* Most of all the knowledge that one owes is much more likely to lead men toward forgiveness of others than standards of illegitimacy for themselves ["On Political Illegitimacy," *Public Policy* (Summer 1971) ; emphasis added.]
>
> Public gratitude, a sense of indebtedness to a shared life of significance and honor, the tradition of sacrifice for the sake of nurturing the public inheritance—most modern interpreters of politics and, we should add, of political theology have refused to recognize

any of this as worthy of analytical attention. Yet interpretations of man and society which do not hold precisely these shared goods, this quality of public ethos, at the center of their attention are premature in their realism and make of man less than common sense knows we are and need to be.[35]

New combinations of technical and planning reason will have to be tried out. Indeed, what is needed now is a new emergence of revolutionary reason, the kind that erupted in the movement from a feudal to a bourgeois age. Perhaps we have no real control over the appearance of such revolutionary gifts in our history. But perhaps we have already seen glimpses of them in some of the earlier notions of the New Left, in the Dubček spring in Czechoslovakia, in the workers' councils amid the Hungarian Revolution, in the emergence of critical management science in American industry.

All of these appearances have in common a new combination of participation and planning, a reversal of the direction of authority from downward to upward and the possibility for a transcendence over narrow self-interest in behalf of an emancipatory interest. They aim at both freedom and belonging. They are far from commanding the future, but they may be anticipations of coming possibilities. They are the "might have beens" of the past, recurring today and crying out for life, not suppression.

The problem of freedom within the context of belonging, which is so difficult for us, looms in our minds, as not only a political and social problem, but also a deeply religious problem. Furthermore, we believe that a clarification of the religious issues that are relevant to this problem is necessary if Americans are to resolve the concrete problems in an adequate manner, so as to realize freedom within belonging. To these issues we now turn.

All that we have suggested about the covenant of belongingness and shalom, as it reshapes our American symbols of the promising and open future and sacrificial dedication, is here brought to its most intense and practical relevance for our American identity. Just as surely as control is shown to be absolutely necessary in our life and just as surely as the caring covenant of our existence is disclosed, just as surely will the straight arrows insist upon their indeterminate freedom which gives them license to shatter control and caring responsibilities. Conversely, there are those, who while insisting upon the straight arrows' freedom for an elite, will only too gladly insist upon control and a repressive belonging for the masses in our society. These two options are typified in the extreme left and the extreme right. The Weatherpeople exemplify the kind of indeterminate freedom that destroys itself like a Roman Candle, while American Nazis like George Lincoln Rockwell embody the free elite who exercise repressive control over others. Or do we need to look to the extremes? The more conventional hyper-individualist and the omnipresent technocrat also embody these two regrettable options of indeterminate freedom and repressive control.

The excruciatingly painful fact is that so many Americans will find ways of escaping the urgency of the freedom/control problem and thus inadvertently advance the cause of either extreme. The resources of the civil religion are spare. Neuhaus and Bellah both hark back to Puritan traditions of communal sensibility that may be brought forward today. We have already described how the Puritan heritage of covenantal sensibilities was dissipated and secularized. Bellah suggests that

> ... the American Indians, and especially those still functioning with some degree of integrity like the Hopi and the Navaho, have much to tell us about the relation between man and natural environment, things that are either missing in the Western biblical tradition or only vestigial among those of its representatives who came to the new world. These are only two of many possible examples. They point out to us that though we are the bearers of a tradition that has its own integrity, it is not a self-sufficient tradition. The survival of all of us on earth today ... depends upon our pooling of all man's cultural resources. If Americans can have any meaning and value in the future it is only a relative value, only as part of a greater encompassing whole.[36]

Those are sentiments that we can concur with fully. But they are only sketchy, and they point out most forcefully that the civil religion is not rich in resources. Bellah adds the traditions of the mid-nineteenth century abolitionist movement and the early Socialist party from 1890 to 1919 that tried to bring economic life under control of the people. Though these movements failed, he says, we can learn from them.

Christian faith suggests that whatever help we get from the failures of the past and from indigenous American Indian or Eastern symbol systems (and we welcome such supportive elements), we do possess in the Jewish and Christian traditions the resources for criticizing our blindness to caring and belongingness and for spelling out what a covenant life might look like. We find these resources in the community of persons who are constituted by their errand into the wilderness to embody the shalom of God, the peace and wholeness that grows out of their interrelatedness to God, land, and to each other. Their future is linked to all people and all nature in God's approaching Kingdom. This life of shalom does not consider that other alternatives are really humane options. The person who denies his belongingness is a no-person, not because he stands under our judgment, but because he has denied his own humanity in his straight-arrow philosophy and piety. It is not enough to say that we stand together or that "no man is an island." We must be certain that we understand how each person is responsible for *caring* for his fellows and for the entire ecosystem in which he or she exists. It is a matter of acknowledging that the networks of our relationships are not launching pads that exist only to be abandoned, that they do not exist just for the purpose of enabling the flight of the manly rockets out of the womb that has given them life. Rather, our relationships are intrinsic to what we are and what we shall become. If there is a launching to take place, it is an entire ecosystem (including all its human beings) that is to be lifted into ascent. If we may be permitted to stretch the imagery, our American civil religion has been generally unattractively "masculine," even sexist, in that everything exists to further the ascent of the masculine American. It is amazing how deeply permeated our American dream is with the notion of the man leaving his supporting matrix (often described in feminine symbols) behind, so that he can pursue the future. As we cited earlier, Frances Fitzgerald has caught this tendency in a vivid phrase: solutions for all problems wait for Americans "like brides" standing on the horizon of the future.[37] In their rightful drive for liberation, it would be tragic if women simply scrambled into that same masculinity, so that the straight arrows became unisexual. It would in the long run be more salutary if, while they move into new roles, women also insisted that their traditional role of caring and binding the world of people into relationship was more than just a role, that it was indeed ontologically grounded. Then, as they drive for human rights and equality, they might insist that their traditional role also must be given a kind of equality, so that their success as human beings would mean a modification of masculinity. To put it crassly, the straight arrows need to be "feminized."

For Westerners there is no tradition that describes our point better than the Hebrew-Christian strand that we have already portrayed. The tradition asserts, "I will lift up my life in the quest for achievement and personal fulfillment, but in so doing, I know that I exist for the sake of my whole world, for my land and for all my brothers and sisters. My achievement is nothing if it is not theirs as well. My personhood is nothing if it is not an increase of their wholeness."

This is a deep lesson to be learned, one that can come only by a complete spiritual regeneration of the American people. The spiritual dimension is necessary for our rebirth as a people, just as the practical social counterpart to the spiritual vision is also necessary for our survival. And if America is in any sense destined to lead the world community, it will do so only in rebirth out of the ashes. We are not all able to design the social, political, economic structures that correspond to the spiritual vision, but we can all live within the framework of the shalom, the wholeness of caring and belonging, that makes us genuinely human. This is the Christian agenda for religious America. It is an agenda that we share with many others. It is an agenda that appears only when—as the Sioux Indians say—the good red road of spiritual understanding crosses the hard black road of worldly difficulties. In the Sioux prayer garden, which is circular in shape, a red road does in fact bisect the garden from south to north, while a black road bisects it from east to west. In the point of intersection a tree grows. That tree is the axis of the world, the place of the Holy. The Sioux believe that every human must reach that point of intersection, and where spiritual understanding meets worldly difficulty, there man will meet the Holy. In this book we have tried to say as clearly as we can that

America is standing at the intersection of those two roads, near the axis of the world. The question is whether Americans can perceive this, whether we can in fact see where we are standing. The red road is the road of the future, the black road is the road of sacrifice. The vision of the Sioux is commensurate in many ways with the Christian view we have set forth. We may say that the religion of the original Americans as well as the religion that the later Americans brought with them focus at this one point. In this focus, the agenda for the spiritual reformation of America, the *defining of America*, stands out in sharp relief.

NOTES

1 Harvey Cox, *The Seduction of the Spirit* (New York: Simon and Schuster, 1973), p. 14.

2 Paul Tillich, *Systematic Theology*, vol. 3 (Chicago: University of Chicago Press, 1967).

3 Langdon Gilkey, *Naming the Whirlwind: The Renewal of God-Language* (Indianapolis and New York: Bobbs-Merrill, 1969).

4 Ibid., p. 281.

5 Ibid., pp. 281 ff.

6 Frances Fitzgerald, *Fire in the Lake* (New York: Vintage Books, 1972), p. 9.

7 Ibid., p. 10.

8 William J. Wolf, *The Almost Chosen People: A Study of the Religion of Abraham Lincoln* (Philadelphia: Pilgrim, 1970), p. 157.

9 Cited in Wolf, pp. 168–169.

10 See Wolf, chap. 10, for an illuminating commentary.

11 Robert Bellah, "Civil Religion in America," *Daedalus* (Winter 1967), p. 10.

12 Cited, in Wolf, p. 13.

13 Richard Neuhaus, *In Defense of People* (New York: Macmillan, 1971), chap. 10.

14 Robert Bellah, "American Civil Religion in the 1970's," in *A Creative Recovery of American Tradition*, ed. W. Taylor Stevenson, *Anglican Theological Review*, Supplementary Series, no. 1 (July 1973), pp. 17–18.

15 Leon Litwack, "The Federal Government and the Free Negro," in *Understanding Negro History*, ed. Dwight Hoover, (Chicago: Quadrangle, 1968), pp. 322–324.

16 Paul Tillich, *Systematic Theology*, vol. 3, pp. 102–106. See also his *Das Dämonische; ein Beitrag zur Sinndeutung der Geschichte* (Tübingen: Mohr, 1926).

[17] Bellah, "Civil Religion in America." See also Sidney Mead, *The Lively Experiment* (New York: Harper & Row, 1963).

[18] See the discussion by John F. Wilson, "The Status of 'Civil Religion' in America," in *The Religion of the Republic*, ed. Elwyn Smith (Philadelphia: Fortress Press, 1971), pp. 1–21.

[19] Ibid., pp. 16–17.

[20] Sidney Ahlstrom, *A Religious History of the American People* (New Haven: Yale University Press, 1972), pp. 1081–1085.

[21] Bellah, "American Civil Religion in the 1970's," p. 14.

[22] Ibid., pp. 15–16.

[23] J. F. Maclear, "The Republic and the Millenium," in *The Religion of the Republic*, ed. Elwyn Smith, pp. 183–216.

[24] Ibid., p. 214.

[25] Bellah, "American Civil Religion in the 1970's," p. 8.

[26] Bellah, "Civil Religion in America," p. 15.

[27] Richard Neuhaus, "The War, the Churches, and Civil Religion," *The Annals of the American Academy of Political and Social Science*, vol. 387 (January 1970), pp. 139–140. See also his "Going Home Again: America after Vietnam," *Worldview 15*, no. 10 (October, 5, 1972), pp. 30–36.

[28] Ibid.

[29] J. Earl Thompson, "The Reform of the Racist Religion of the Republic," in *The Religion of the Republic*, ed. Smith, p. 268.

[30] For a summary of the complex materials and interpretations pertaining to sacrifice in the Hebrew-Christian tradition, see the following: H. Ringgren, *Sacrifice in the Bible* (London: Lutterworth, 1962); Markus Barth, *Was Christ's Death a Sacrifice? Scottish Journal of Theology*, Occasional Papers, no. 9 (1961).

[31] Pierre Teilhard de Chardin, *Science and Christ* (New York: Harper & Row, 1968), especially chaps. 3, 7, 8.

[32] Martin Heidegger, *Being and Time* (New York: Harper & Row, 1962), p. 439.

[33] See Wolfhart Pannenberg, *Theology and the Kingdom of God* (Philadelphia: Westminster, 1969); Carl Braaten, *The Future of God* (New York: Harper & Row, 1969); Jürgen Moltmann, *Theology of Hope: On the Ground and the Implications of a Christian Eschatology*, trans. James W. Leitch (New York: Harper & Row, 1967); Klaus Koch, *The Rediscovery of Apocalyptic* (Naperville, Ill.: Allenson, 1972).

[34] Quoted in Richard Neuhaus, "Liberation Theology and the Captivities of Jesus," *Worldview* 16, no. 6 (June 1973), p. 48.

[35] John C. Raines, "Theodicy and Politics," *Worldview* 16 (April 1973), p. 46.

[36] Bellah, "American Civil Religion in the 1970's," p. 19.

[37] See note 6, this chapter.